I0821062

THE WORLD'S BEST
BEACHES

Stefanie Waldek

Table of contents

EUROPE

SOUTH AMERICA

NORTH & CENTRAL AMERICA

AFRICA

ANTARCTICA

Hyams Beach in Jervis Bay, New South Wales, has exceptionally soft white silica sand. Hyams Beach is found on the southern shores of the splendid Jervis Bay Marine Park, and its calm waters are ideal for swimming, snorkeling, and stand-up paddleboarding. A few animals you might see while you're here: bottlenose dolphins, fur seals, and little penguins. And during whale migration season, from late May to late September, you might even see humpback whales. Birders shouldn't miss the Hyams Beach trail, a designated "bird spotter's walk."

	HYAMS BEACH	Jervis Bay, New South Wales	AUSTRALIA

When you think of beaches in Australia, Bondi Beach probably comes to mind. This is one of Sydney's main tourist attractions, but you'd better believe the locals love it too. People come here to surf, swim (particularly in the iconic Bondi Icebergs Swimming Club), and sun, but they also come to stroll the Bondi to Coogee coastal walk, which offers stunning views of the coastline. The surrounding area is packed with cafés, bars, and shops—not to mention the Bondi Skate Park—so there's plenty to do off the beach, too.

	BONDI BEACH	Sydney, New South Wales	AUSTRALIA

	LUCKY BAY	Cape Le Grand National Park, Western Australia	AUSTRALIA

A 2017 scientific study found that Lucky Bay in Western Australia's Cape Le Grand National Park has the whitest sand of all Australian beaches. If you want to visit the beach with this unusual superlative, you'll have to make a bit of a trek to get there. The closest town is Esperance, which is a 45-minute drive from Lucky Bay, and Esperance itself is an eight-hour drive from Perth (or an hour-and-a-half flight). But the white sands sure are worth it—especially because there are resident kangaroos that enjoy the beach, too.

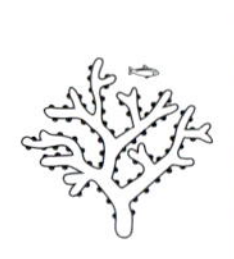

CORAL BAY	Western Australia	AUSTRALIA

At Coral Bay in Western Australia, it's actually less about the beach and more about what's just off it. Put on your snorkel mask, step into the warm water, and put your face down—you're looking at the UNESCO-designated Ningaloo Reef, a fringing reef that's exceptionally close to the shore. It is an overwhelming explosion of color down there in the coral gardens, which are absolutely teeming with life. This region is also known for whale sharks, manta rays, sea turtles, and even dugongs. After a few hours of snorkeling through this marine wonderland, haul yourself out onto the beach for a well-deserved nap under an umbrella.

Freycinet National Park is home to the iconic Wineglass Bay, which is one of, if not *the* most photographed places in all of Tasmania. Surrounded by rugged granite peaks and native bushland, Wineglass Bay is a haven for nature lovers and adventure seekers. The beach is accessible via a scenic hike that offers breathtaking views from the Wineglass Bay Lookout, and visitors can enjoy swimming, kayaking, and bushwalking here. To maximize your time at Wineglass Bay, stay at the nearby camping grounds at Coles Bay. If you're looking for an easier trip to the beach, consider booking a scenic cruise.

	WINEGLASS BAY	Freycinet National Park, Tasmania	AUSTRALIA

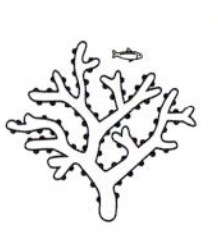

WHITEHAVEN BEACH	Whitsunday Island	AUSTRALIA

Whitehaven Beach might just be the world's most quintessential beach. Located on Whitsunday Island in the heart of the Great Barrier Reef, it is world-renowned for its powdery white silica sand that's exceptionally soft—and it doesn't heat up under the sun! Who's in for a long walk? Whitehaven Beach stretches more than four miles and is backed by lush hills; you can hike up to the Hill Inlet lookout to see the best view of the swirling white sands and turquoise waters blending together. The beach is accessible only by boat, helicopter, or seaplane—if you choose one of the latter, you can skip the lookout and get a bird's-eye view on your way in.

You'd be easily forgiven for thinking the extraordinary white-sand beaches along Lake McKenzie are ocean beaches, but they are, indeed, on the edge of a freshwater lake. Lake McKenzie, located on UNESCO-listed K'gari (formerly Fraser Island) in Queensland, is a "perched" lake, which means it sits well above sea level—and it's fed only by rainwater, not groundwater or a river. But it does have that white silica sand that's so popular across Australian beaches. The lake is perfect for swimming, and there are camping facilities nearby.

LAKE MCKENZIE	K'gari, Queensland	AUSTRALIA

	SHELL BEACH	Shark Bay, Western Australia	AUSTRALIA

Can you guess what you might find on this beach? Yes, shells, and lots of them. Shell Beach, located in Western Australia's Shark Bay, is made of billions (or maybe even trillions) of tiny shells from the Fragum cockle, a bivalve mollusk. The beach stretches on for dozens of miles, and in some places, the shell deposits are more than 30 feet deep. It's certainly one of the more unusual beaches out there, but this UNESCO World Heritage Site is something to behold. The water is rather interesting here, too—it's extremely salty, so you'll float easily in it.

BYRON BAY	New South Wales	AUSTRALIA

Byron Bay is a famous coastal community in New South Wales, Australia, and it's home to some of the state's best beaches. There are numerous ways to enjoy them, from kayaks to horses to surfboards, or simply your own two feet. Or you can get up in the air, taking a hot air balloon ride to see the beaches from above—or ogle them as you skydive. If you're looking for the easiest beach to get to, that'd be Main Beach, in the center of town. Want to surf? Make for Lennox Head, a National Surfing Reserve. If it's dramatic scenery you seek, make your way out to Little Wategos, the most easterly beach in Australia.

For the perfect romantic beach getaway, make your way to Aitutaki in the Cook Islands, home to the Aitutaki Lagoon Private Island Resort. This adults-only property has 36 bungalows spread across "the world's most beautiful lagoon," as it calls its home. It truly is beautiful, with white-sand beaches along its 15 *motus* (islets) and vibrant coral reefs in the heart of the lagoon. Laze the day away on the sand, spend a few hours snorkeling, or ride your bike around the grounds—no matter where you look, you're sure to be greeted by a postcard-perfect view.

	**AITUTAKI LAGOON**	Aitutaki	COOK ISLANDS

	**NATADOLA BEACH**	Viti Levu	FIJI

Fiji's main island of Viti Levu is home to one of the island nation's best beaches: Natadola Beach. The soft sand meanders along for a mile and a half, making for a lovely, leisurely stroll—take a dip in the aquamarine sea when you need a break from the sun. For more active pursuits, try your hand at surfing, or go horseback riding—locals bring their horses here for visitors to ride along the shore. While the beach is open to the public, it's also home to a luxury resort, if you're interested in making this your home base in Fiji.

The Yasawa Island group in Fiji comprises 20 volcanic islands with dramatic peaks and white-sand beaches—it's impossible to pick only one beach as this region's best. Throughout the islands are various accommodations ranging from boutique resorts to rustic bungalows, catering to all kinds of travelers. But generally speaking, the travelers happiest here are the ones looking to get out into nature. Explore the islands' limestone caves, snorkel off the pristine beaches, or even swim with manta rays. Yasawa means "heaven" in Fijian, and these islands really are a natural paradise.

	YASAWA ISLANDS	—	FIJI

	MATIRA BEACH	Bora Bora	FRENCH POLYNESIA

Bora Bora is filled with beautiful beaches, but many of them are reserved for private resorts. But then there's Matira Beach, the only public beach on the island, and one of the largest, spanning nearly two miles. Located on the southern tip of the island, Matira Beach is a favorite for both locals and tourists seeking a tranquil, picturesque setting—it's a particularly good spot for families, as the water is shallow and calm here, which is perfect for snorkeling. There are a handful of casual beach cafés along the sand, but otherwise this is a quiet, relaxing place to spend the day.

	KOEKOHE BEACH	Otago Coast	NEW ZEALAND

If you're road-tripping along the Otago coast of New Zealand, be sure to add Koekohe Beach, also known as Moeraki Beach, to your itinerary. This beach is famous for the Moeraki Boulders, large stones that are remarkably and somewhat eerily spherical, that are spread across the sand. These boulders, some as large as six feet in diameter, are thought to have formed up to 65 million years ago, as pebbles accreted mud and calcite concretions over the millennia. But Māori legend suggests that the boulders were once gourds or eel baskets that washed ashore from a shipwrecked canoe.

CATHEDRAL COVE	Coromandel Peninsula	NEW ZEALAND

Your journey to Cathedral Cove will begin at another beach, Hahei Beach, from which you'll walk an hour along a clifftop before descending to this iconic rock formation on the beach. Located on the Coromandel Peninsula, Cathedral Cove's main attraction is a cathedral-like natural stone arch, which spans a scenic beach dotted with pōhutukawa trees. Of course, there are other ways to get here too—like hopping on a 10-minute water taxi or paddling a kayak over. Don't forget your snorkel, as the surrounding waters are part of the Te Whanganui-o-Hei Marine Reserve.

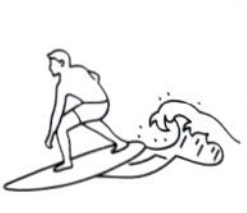

	MURIWAI BEACH	Auckland Region	NEW ZEALAND

Just 45 minutes outside of Auckland, Muriwai Beach feels a world apart from the city. There are nearly 40 miles of black-sand beaches along the rugged coastline in this popular weekend getaway destination, so there's plenty of space for everyone. Muriwai is particularly known for its surf—it's a great place to learn as a beginner, though more advanced surfers will have fun here, too. And given the winds here, it's also a popular kite-surfing spot. For a more relaxed activity, consider visiting the gannet colony at Otakamiro Point; the birds are in residence from August to March.

On the northern tip of New Zealand's South Island, Wharariki Beach draws those looking to experience the rugged beauty of nature—and photographers looking to capture the two archway islands just off the shore. To get there, you'll want to take the Wharariki Beach Walk, which traverses farmland and forest before bringing you to the beach, where you can continue exploring tide pools and sand dunes, particularly at low tide. Keep in mind that the waves here can be quite big, so it's best to leave the swimming to the resident seal population.

	**WHARARIKI BEACH**	Nelson Tasman	NEW ZEALAND

	**BUSHY BEACH**	Oamaru	NEW ZEALAND

At Bushy Beach, near Oamaru on New Zealand's South Island, it's all about the penguins. This is one of the few places you can see the rare, endangered yellow-eyed penguin, or *hoiho*, in the wild. It's estimated that there are fewer than 150 breeding pairs on the South Island, a few of which make their nest here—as the evening approaches, you might spot a few returning to the beach from a day hunting at sea. Because the penguins are protected, you'll have to stay at the top of the cliffs to see them. Camp out at one of the overlooks during sunset and bring a pair of binoculars to get a good look at these rare penguins.

	NINETY MILE BEACH	Aupōuri Peninsula	NEW ZEALAND

Guess how long the North Island's Ninety Mile Beach is? If you guessed 90 miles, you'd be wrong. It's just about 55 miles long. And no one is really sure why it's named what it is! But the beach's Māori name is a bit more accurate: Te Oneroa-a-Tōhē, or the long beach of Tōhē. Today, the long, flat beach is officially an unpaved, scenic highway, though it's advised that you drive it only in a 4WD vehicle. You can surf here, however, and you can fish—surfcasting is a particularly popular sport on the beach, and there's even an annual fishing competition here.

Karekare Beach, located less than an hour's drive from Auckland along the Tasman Sea, is famous for its black sand, powerful surf, and dramatic cliffs. While it's long been a popular day trip for Aucklanders, the beach gained international fame after being featured in the 1993 film *The Piano*. As with many of the beaches on Auckland's wild west coast, surfing is a popular activity here, but Karekare Beach is also a great spot to take in the area's rugged beauty from the shore on a scenic walk. Just a five-minute walk off the beach, in the subtropical rainforest, are the beautiful Karekare Falls.

KAREKARE BEACH	Auckland Region	NEW ZEALAND

The volcanic island of Savai'i is the largest in Samoa, and it's home to numerous beaches, not least of which is Manase Beach. White sand, turquoise waters, vibrant coral reefs—yes, this is your classic tropical beach, and that is reason enough to visit it! What makes Manase Beach stand out, though, is the fact that it's lined with beach *fale*, or traditional houses, that you can rent for your visit here. Bring your snorkel gear, as it's not uncommon to see sea turtles all around Savai'i, but especially at Manase Beach.

	**MANASE BEACH**	Savai'i	SAMOA

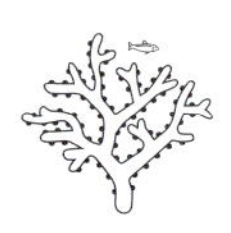

FUNAFUTI ATOLL	—	TUVALU

The small island nation of Tuvalu comprises nine coral islands, the largest of which is Funafuti Atoll. Some 30 islets surround a large lagoon, and many of them have beautiful little beaches. The main islet, Fongafale, is home to the village of Vaiaku, and the easily accessible Funafuti Lagoon Beach. But perhaps one of the most beautiful is Funafala Beach on Funafala, which has soft, white sand and shallow seas—you might even see sea turtles swim by. For a more secluded experience, take a boat out to Tefonufala Beach, on a tiny islet that's hardly visited.

	ETON BEACH	Éfaté	VANUATU

Vanuatu is another Pacific island nation known for its breathtaking beaches, which can be found across its 83 islands. On the main island, Éfaté, you'll find Eton Beach, one of the more secluded stretches of sand, some 45 minutes from Port Vila, the country's commercial center. It's a family-friendly spot adjacent to the jungle, with plenty of shallow tidal pools, grottoes, and coves to explore. Just down the road is the famous Blue Lagoon, a popular swimming spot that you should add to your itinerary if you make it out this way.

CHAMPAGNE BEACH

Espiritu Santo

VANUATU

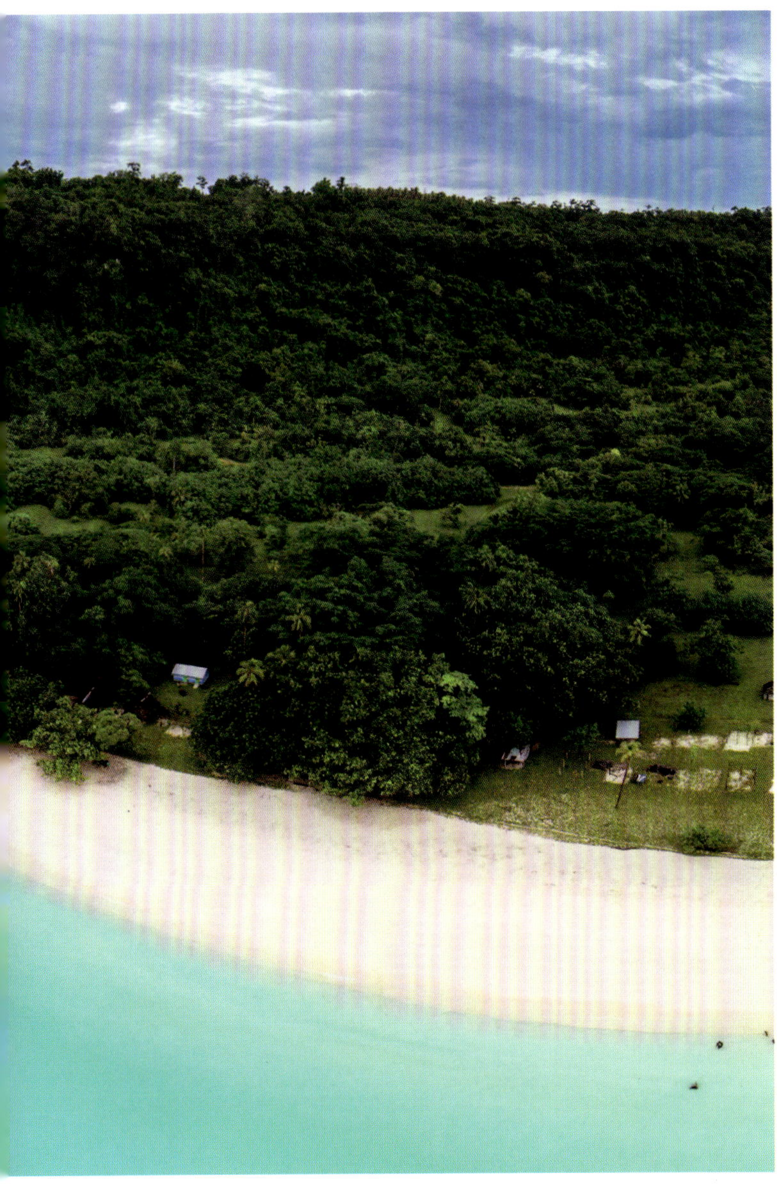

Espiritu Santo's Champagne Beach is the most famous beach in Vanuatu; with soft white sand fringed by lush foliage, it's a scenic spot that's particularly popular with cruise ship guests visiting the island. Its name is derived from a unique phenomenon where volcanic gas bubbles rise to the surface of the sea during low tide, the effervescence tickling the toes of anyone wading through or snorkeling in the turquoise water. While it might not be the most secluded beach in Vanuatu, it sure is a pretty one.

	LONNOC BEACH	Espiritu Santo	VANUATU

Just a short walk from Champagne Beach is Lonnoc Beach, a quieter but no less beautiful spot. If you're not visiting on a cruise ship, this is a great place to stay, as there are bungalows and lodges along the white-sand beach. But day visitors can enjoy Lonnoc Beach's tranquility, too, especially those looking to get away from the crowds at Champagne Beach. This beach has its own little oddity, too—an underwater spring introduces fresh water to the sea, and you can feel the temperature difference between the fresh water and the salt water as you're swimming here. Lonnoc Beach is a particularly good spot for kayaking, as the waters are quite calm here.

	LAZY BEACH	Koh Rong Samloem	CAMBODIA

There are many crowded beaches in Southeast Asia—Cambodia's Lazy Beach is not one of them. This private beach on Koh Rong Samloem is open only to guests of the Lazy Beach resort, which has rustic thatched-roof bungalows along the sand for a laid-back getaway. When you're not lazing the day away on the golden sand, you can swim out to the house reef and go snorkeling or hike the inland trails to the jungle. If you're seeking a bit more entertainment, you can hike over to the other side of the island, where there are plenty more resorts. But for a secluded getaway, it doesn't get better than Lazy Beach.

	**YALONG BAY**	Hainan Island	CHINA

At nearly five miles long, Yalong Bay has more than enough room for everyone on its white sands. This beach on Hainan Island outside of Sanya City is lined with luxury resorts, solidifying the destination as a popular vacation spot for both domestic and international visitors. The bay's crystal-clear waters are perfect for swimming, diving, and watersports—book a trip out to the Sanya Coral Reef National Marine Nature Reserve for the best wildlife spotting—while the surrounding area offers hiking through forests. Or if you simply want to relax on the beach, there's nothing wrong with that! From your beach lounger, you can enjoy views of the surrounding mountains and the sea.

VARKALA BEACH	Kerala	INDIA

The Indian state of Kerala is famous for its beaches; not least among them is Varkala Beach, also known as Papanasam Beach. Overlooking the Arabian Sea, this beach is special for the pink laterite cliffs that surround it—it's the only place in India where cliffs abut the Arabian Sea, and as such, the Geological Survey of India has designated it a geological monument. The beach has a spiritual component, as tradition suggests the spring within the cliffs has healing waters. In fact, that's why there's a 2,000-year-old Hindu temple built atop the cliffs: the Janardhana Swamy Temple.

	PALOLEM BEACH	Goa	INDIA

Like Kerala, the Indian state of Goa is also known for its beaches; up north, you'll find particularly lively resort destinations, while in the south, the atmosphere is a bit more laid-back. Palolem Beach is in the south, but it has just enough liveliness to keep you entertained during your beach vacation here. The crescent-shaped beach is lined with colorful beach huts, home to restaurants, bars, and lodging, and its calm waters are perfect for swimming and kayaking. Head out on a boat trip to look for dolphins, or sail over to the more secluded Butterfly Beach nearby.

RADHANAGAR BEACH	Havelock Island, Andaman and Nicobar Islands	INDIA

The Andaman and Nicobar Islands are an Indian union territory located off the coast of Myanmar, and they're known for their lush rainforests, rich biodiversity, and, of course, beautiful beaches. One of the top beaches in the region is Radhanagar Beach, known locally as Beach No. 7, on Havelock Island, where white sands stretch between dense rainforest and calm, blue seas. Walk to the northern reaches of the beach and you'll find Neil's Cove, a secluded, smaller beach that's particularly photogenic, with its shallow, teal lagoon fed by freshwater streams. But be wary of the crocodiles in the inlets here!

PINK BEACH	Komodo Island	INDONESIA

Yes, this beach on Komodo Island is known for its namesake feature: pink sand. The hue comes from a combination of white sand and red coral fragments, and if you snorkel out into the turquoise waters, you can actually see the red coral along the reef. The beach, also known as Pantai Merah, is located on Komodo Island and is part of Komodo National Park, home of the famous Komodo dragon. If you're planning a trip here, aim to visit during the dry season, which runs from April through December—sunny skies bring out the pink color brilliantly.

BROKEN BEACH	Nusa Penida Island, Bali	INDONESIA

It might not have the most appealing name, but Bali's Broken Beach is an impressive sight. The beach, also known as Pasih Uug Beach, is located at the bottom of a sinkhole-like formation within limestone cliffs. From the air, it has a circular appearance, and as you approach the edge, you'll notice a beautiful natural arch opening up to the sea. Waves roll through, churning up the waters along the sand at the base of the rock formation. It's a spectacular scene, but there is something visitors should know—you can't actually get down to the beach. But you can certainly enjoy it from the clifftop nonetheless.

LONG SAND BEACH	Labengki Island	INDONESIA

If you want to get away from it all, you can head off the beaten path at Long Sand Beach, also known as Pantai Pasir Panjang, on Indonesia's Labengki Island. As its name suggests, it's the longest beach on this remote island, located off the coast of Sulawesi—all that's here are trees, white sand, and pristine waters. As some visitors put it, the remote wilderness feels like Jurassic Park. Labengki is a little-visited destination by both domestic and international tourists, and, in fact, there's no way to get here unless you charter a trip by a local operator. Is it worth the endeavor? You'll just have to visit to find out.

FRIWEN ISLAND	Raja Ampat Archipelago	INDONESIA

Located in Indonesia's Raja Ampat Archipelago, the tiny island of Friwen is an idyllic beach getaway—especially for snorkelers and divers. The island is surrounded by coral reefs, and just off the island is the Friwenbonda, or Friwen Wall, a limestone tower that's a particularly popular snorkel and dive site. But when you're not in the water, you can relax on the white-sand beach and listen to the waves gently lap against the sand. Friwen's only accommodations are homestays, which are a great way to get to know a welcoming local family—they might even serve up a beachfront barbecue for guests.

WALAKIRI BEACH

Sumba Island

INDONESIA

There's no shortage of picture-perfect beaches on Indonesia's Sumba Island; these beaches are known for their white sands and dramatic cliffs. But one of the most photogenic beaches on the island is Walakiri Beach, known for its grove of dwarf mangroves. At sunset, the trees are beautifully silhouetted—photographers flock here when the sun is setting and the tide is low, the reflections of the gnarled trees adding to the drama of the scene. This isn't a particularly swimmable beach, though, so it's best for strolling among the trees and sunbathing rather than snorkeling.

SHIRAHAMA BEACH	Kansai	JAPAN

You've probably heard of sister cities, but what about sister beaches? This white-sand beach in Japan's Kansai region is a sister beach to Hawaii's famous Waikiki Beach. Shirahama opens the earliest of all of Honshu's beaches, heralding the start of summer each season. While its white sands are undoubtedly beautiful, they're not actually native to Japan—the grains have been imported from Australia, as the original beach has long since eroded away. Still, this family-friendly beach is a delight to visit, particularly during the summer fireworks shows. While pyrotechnics are common all summer long, the biggest festival is on August 10, and it's accompanied by a slew of food stalls along the beach.

SUNAYAMA BEACH	Miyako Island	JAPAN

Sunayama Beach, located on Miyako Island in Okinawa Prefecture, isn't a particularly large beach, but it sure is a pretty one. Its name means "sand mountain beach," which is appropriate given the fact you have to descend a sand dune to reach it. At the base, you'll find a natural rock arch that's the subject of many a photograph. Set up a towel, relax on the white-sand beach, and take a cooling dip in the pretty blue sea—Sunayama Beach is a lovely place to spend a few relaxing hours. If it's snorkeling you're after, visit the nearby Nakanoshima Beach, another small beach known for its lively reef.

	**MIHO-NO-MATSUBARA**	Miho Peninsula	JAPAN

Miho-no-Matsubara is not a tropical beach, but it's a stunning one nonetheless. The black-sand beach is lined with more than 30,000 pine trees, making for incredibly peaceful strolls along the water. Oh, and the beach has an iconic view of Mount Fuji; it's part of the Mount Fuji UNESCO World Heritage Site. In 1915, Miho-no-Matsubara was voted one of the New Three Views of Japan, cementing it as one of the most picturesque landscapes in the entire country. It should come as no surprise that master artist Utagawa Hiroshige captured the landscape in one of his ukiyo-e woodblock prints.

	**PANTAI CENANG**	Langkawi Island	MALAYSIA

Pantai Cenang might just be the flagship beach of Langkawi Island, the largest island in Malaysia's Langkawi Archipelago. This isn't a place for solitude—it's a bustling beach lined with resorts, bars, clubs, restaurants, and shops, entertaining visitors by day and night. Of course, the 1.2-mile-long beach is lovely in itself, so if you don't want to participate in any of the landside activities, you don't have to! There are, however, watersports rentals for ocean activities, whether that's banana boating, parasailing, jet skiing, or good old-fashioned snorkeling. For a more secluded beach, try Tanjung Rhu Beach on the other side of the island.

Tanjung Bungah was once a quiet suburb of George Town on Malaysia's Penang Island, but it's becoming more and more urban as development continues. It remains a popular beach destination, however, with its main public beach now lined with high-rise condos. Overall, Tanjung Bungah Beach is less crowded than some of the other beaches on the island, which is pretty impressive given its densely populated area—it makes for the perfect afternoon excursion from downtown George Town. At one end of the beach, you'll find the Tanjung Bungah Floating Mosque, which isn't actually floating, but rather is built on stilts. When the tide is high, though, you can see the illusion.

TANJUNG BUNGAH BEACH

Penang Island

MALAYSIA

BAROS ISLAND — MALDIVES

It'd be easy to fill an entire book with only Maldivian beaches, as the island nation is absolutely packed with gorgeous spots. But I'll limit my selection to just a couple of beautiful spots. First up is Baros Island, one of the Maldives' original resorts, opened in 1973. While it has a number of overwater bungalows, beach lovers might prefer the beach villas instead—they open directly onto the sand. Definitely don your complimentary snorkel mask here, as the island is famous for its house reef, one of the largest in the Maldives.

FULHADHOO ISLAND	Baa Atoll	MALDIVES

While many Maldivian islands are private resorts, Fulhadhoo is one of the inhabited islands with a small local community, technically located in the Baa Atoll, but far from most tourist destinations. But there are a smattering of locally owned guesthouses and hotels here—smaller, more budget-friendly ones than the big commercial resorts. Yet you'll find the same white-sand beaches here as you would at the resorts! The main beach is more than half a mile long, and off it, you'll find a house reef for snorkeling and diving (there is a dive center on the island).

	NACPAN BEACH	Palawan Island	PHILIPPINES

Nacpan Beach is an easy day trip from El Nido on Palawan Island—it's about a 45-minute drive from the town center. Known for its wide stretch of golden sand and crystal-clear waters, Nacpan is perfect for swimming, sunbathing, and relaxing under the coconut trees. And it's generally away from the big crowds, as only a few small resorts, guesthouses, and glampsites provide accommodation on this beach. Walk to the end, and you'll find Nacpan's "twin beach," Calitang. It's much smaller than Nacpan, though, so it's not so much of a twin. That said, it's just as beautiful!

WHITE BEACH	Boracay	PHILIPPINES

White Beach on the resort island of Boracay is one of the most famous beaches in the world, known for its powdery white sand. The beach stretches for 2.5 miles and is lined with hotels, shops, restaurants, and bars, making it a lively and popular destination. White Beach is divided into three sections —Station 1, Station 2, and Station 3— each offering different vibes, from the serenity of luxury resorts to the excitement of beach volleyball to the party-all-night-long atmosphere of beach bars and clubs. But no matter the atmosphere, one thing remains the same along White Beach: the beauty of nature.

	KHALAKTYRSKY BEACH	Kamchatka Peninsula	RUSSIA

Russia's remote Kamchatka Peninsula on the Pacific Ocean's Ring of Fire might not be tropical, but it sure does have some exquisite rugged beaches. Khalaktyrsky Beach, located about a 40-minute drive from the city of Petropavlovsk-Kamchatsky, is a volcanic black-sand beach that's popular with surfers—in all seasons. Yes, even in the snowy winter, you'll find intrepid surfers in the water. The beach is home to the Snowave Kamchatka Surf Camp, which is open all year long, so you can always take a lesson here. Just be prepared for fairly rugged facilities, as this isn't a developed beach, which is all the better to enjoy its natural state.

Located in the northern Sri Lankan city of Trincomalee, also known as Trinco, Uppuveli Beach is a quieter beach compared with some of the resort destinations elsewhere in the country. Though visitors are warmly welcome to enjoy the honey-colored sands—there are a number of laid-back hotels and lodges here—Uppuveli still has a very local atmosphere. If you make the trek to this beach, don't miss the chance to visit Trinco's cultural and historic sites, such as the Koneswaram Temple and Fort Frederick. If you decide to go for a swim at Uppuveli Beach, be mindful of the currents, as they can get quite strong.

	**UPPUVELI BEACH**	Trincomalee	SRI LANKA

Fernando's Bar

Koggala Beach is the longest in Sri Lanka, spanning more than two miles. But despite this, it's surprisingly under the radar — there aren't usually large crowds here. That means it's a perfect beach for lounging unbothered. And while it isn't the most popular surf spot in Sri Lanka, there are surfable waves here, so if you're looking to get away from the hordes, this is a good spot. The town of Koggala is a quaint little area; it's the hometown of Sinhalese author Martin Wickramasinghe, and there's a museum here dedicated to his life and work.

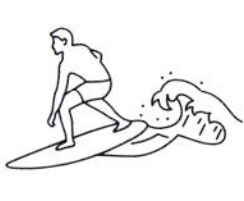

KOGGALA BEACH

Koggala

SRI LANKA

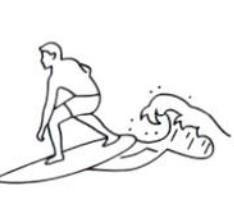

	HIRIKETIYA BEACH	South Coast	SRI LANKA

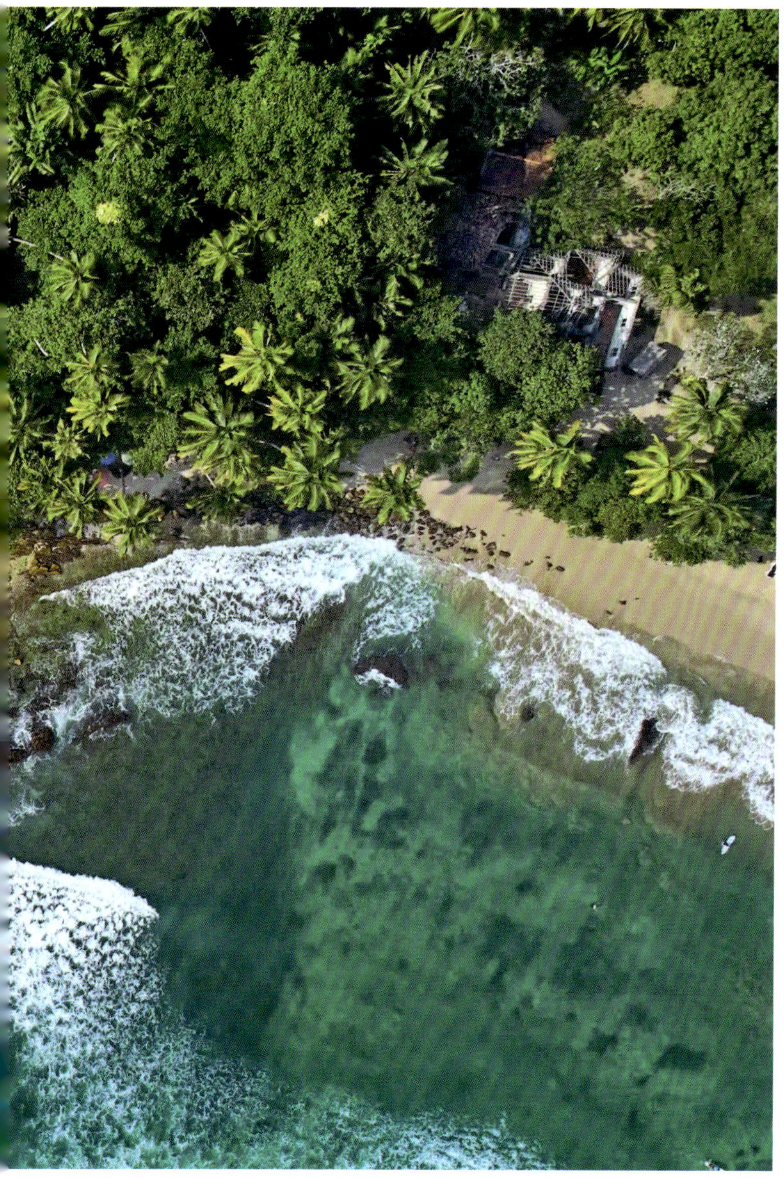

Hiriketiya Beach, also known as Hiri, is located in a small, horseshoe-shaped cove bordered by jungle on one side and good surf on the other. So, yes, you can certainly expect to find surfers here—lots of them, when the swell is good. But there are also many observers, yogis, and sun worshippers on the beach, so you won't feel left out if you're not hitting the waves. There's very much a chill, carefree vibe here, and that draws in many slow travelers who want to spend extended time here. But the secret about Hiri is definitely out, so the short-term visitors are growing in number.

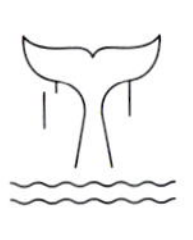	**MIRISSA BEACH**	South Coast	SRI LANKA

Mirissa Beach is not a hidden gem, but it is a gem nonetheless. It's one of the most popular beach destinations in Sri Lanka, thanks to the golden sand, blue-green waters, and scenic island just inside the bay, which you can walk to via a sandbar at low tide. And that's not to mention the beach bars, restaurants, and clubs that line the shore. Mirissa is also a popular spot for whale watching, with boat tours offering the chance to see blue whales—the largest animal on Earth today—between November and April.

	MAYA BAY	Hat Noppharat Thara-Mu Ko Phi Phi National Park	THAILAND

Maya Bay in Thailand's Hat Noppharat Thara-Mu Ko Phi Phi National Park is just so dazzling that it was scouted by Hollywood, becoming something of a celebrity in its own right thanks to its role in the 2000 film *The Beach* starring Leonardo DiCaprio. The bay is surrounded by towering limestone cliffs, creating a stunning natural amphitheater with soft white sand and clear turquoise waters—it's not hard to see why this location was chosen for the film. Unfortunately, its fame became too much. Overtourism damaged the ecosystem, but fortunately not permanently. The Thai government closed the spot for years, allowing nature to heal, before letting visitors back in smaller numbers.

AO NANG	Krabi Province	THAILAND

It's impossible to pick the best beach in Ao Nang, Thailand, so the entire region around this coastal town is getting a full entry in this book. Once a sleepy backpacker destination, Ao Nang is now a tourism hotspot, and its many beaches are certainly a big draw. Ao Nang Beach is the main stretch here, and while it's a hub with restaurants, bars, and shops, it's not as dramatic as some of the nearby beaches, such as Phra Nang Cave Beach and Railay Beach, which feature massive limestone cliffs. Ao Nang is also a good hub for exploring the Phi Phi Islands, as many boat tours depart from town.

The island of Koh Pha-Ngan might be renowned for its Full Moon Parties, but if that's not your scene, there's still a great reason to visit the destination: its beaches. One of the best is Thong Nai Pan, comprising a pair of secluded beaches, Thong Nai Pan Noi and Thong Nai Pan Yai, with a handful of laid-back luxury resorts and boutique hotels. At the edge of Thong Nai Pan Yai is a hill with a scenic overlook—and the 2C Bar—that gives you a bird's-eye view of the golden sands. These beaches are both family-friendly and romantic, so they make for an ideal vacation destination for all sorts of travelers who aren't looking to indulge in Koh Pha-Ngan's party scene.

	**THONG NAI PAN**	Koh Pha-Ngan	THAILAND

PANVIMAN RESORT

Sairee Beach is a busy place. This is the longest and most popular beach on Koh Tao, an island with a reputation for its dive scene—with dozens of dive shops along the beach, it's easy to either get your diving certification or book an excursion if you're already an experienced diver. But for the non-divers, this is a paradise for eating and drinking beachside. In the evening, the beach transforms into a lively scene with fire shows and nightlife. By day, however, you'll find sunbathers and swimmers on this beach.

	SAIREE BEACH	Koh Tao	THAILAND

Drive 1.5 hours south of Antalya, and you'll reach the village of Çirali, a quiet destination known for its lush hills filled with pine and citrus trees. The largely undeveloped beach is part of a protected area due to its importance as a nesting site for endangered loggerhead sea turtles, but visitors are welcome to sunbathe and swim here outside of nesting season. The nearby ruins of the ancient city of Olympos and the Chimaera, a series of natural eternal flames, add to the appeal of the area, which has a delightfully tranquil atmosphere.

	ÇIRALI BEACH	Çirali	TURKEY

The resort town of Çeşme near Izmir, Turkey, is home to Ilica Beach, known for its fine white sand and warm, shallow waters. Interestingly, the water isn't warmed due to the sun or hot air temperatures, but rather natural hot springs that bubble up in certain areas of the sea, creating warm patches that visitors can enjoy while swimming. The area around Ilica Beach is filled with luxury hotels, restaurants, and beach clubs, offering plenty of amenities for travelers. Windsurfing is also popular here, with several schools available for beginners and experts alike.

	ILICA BEACH	Çeşme	TURKEY

Towering palm trees, powdery white sand, calm waters—this is Sao Beach on Vietnam's Phú Quốc island. Sao Beach is less developed than other beaches on the island, offering a more peaceful and serene atmosphere. But there are a handful of beachside restaurants and bars that provide fresh seafood and drinks, as well as a few watersports rental companies, so there's still plenty to do throughout the day. Sao Beach is a popular spot for day-trippers coming from the port city of An Thới, located just about three miles away, but there are some accommodations here if you'd like to prolong your visit.

SAO BEACH	Phú Quốc	VIETNAM

	ZLATNI RAT	Brač	CROATIA

Zlatni Rat, also known as the Golden Horn or the Golden Cape, is one of Croatia's most famous—and certainly most photogenic—beaches. Its name alludes to why: the V-shaped spit of golden sand juts off the end of the island of Brač, its shape constantly shifting with the wind and tides. The beach is a hotspot for windsurfing, thanks to those winds that shape it, but is also favored by those looking to sunbathe or simply have an afternoon picnic. Surrounded by a lush pine grove, the area offers plenty of shade and scenic walking paths, while the nearby town of Bol provides easy access to restaurants, cafés, and historical sites.

NISSI BEACH	Ayia Napa	CYPRUS

Located near Ayia Napa on the southeastern coast of Cyprus, Nissi Beach is known for its golden sand and vibrant waters—and its summer beach parties. The beach is particularly popular with young crowds for this clubby atmosphere, which can be found at Nissi Bay Beach Bar. But move down the 2,000-foot-long beach, and it becomes a more family-friendly scene, with amenities like sunbeds and umbrellas. Nissi Beach is named for the islet Nissi just off the beach, which you can swim or wade to, depending on the tide.

The Calanques are a series of stunning limestone cliffs and coves that stretch along the Mediterranean coast between Marseille and Cassis in southern France. There are quite a few narrow inlets with steep rock faces here, some of which have pebble or sandy beaches nestled into them—perhaps the most famous is Calanque d'En-Vau. To get here, you'll have to hike 45 minutes on foot, or you can book a boat tour. Despite being a touch difficult to get to, Calanque d'En-Vau draws quite large crowds, so don't expect to be the only person on this beach!

	CALANQUE D'EN-VAU	The Calanques	FRANCE

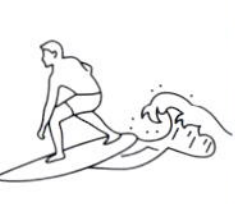

SAINT-MALO

Brittany

FRANCE

Saint-Malo on the northern coast of Brittany is a historic walled city surrounded by beautiful sandy beaches. The town's main beach, the Grande Plage du Sillon, stretches for nearly two miles along the wall, offering plenty of space for beachgoers to relax, swim, and enjoy watersports such as windsurfing and kitesurfing. Another favorite beach here is the Plage de Bon-Secours, known for its seawater swimming pool, built in the 1930s. The tides at Saint-Malo are dramatic, with the sea retreating far out during low tide, revealing rock pools and islands that can be explored on foot.

	DEAUVILLE	Normandy	FRANCE

A Victorian-era resort town meets Hollywood glamour at Deauville in Normandy, often referred to as the "Queen of the Norman Beaches." The area was once filled with marshes, but in the late 19th century, they were drained to create a luxurious seaside resort, with a golden beach and chic hotels. Today, Deauville is not just a beach town; it's a high-end hub with hotels, casinos, and horse-racing events drawing visitors from all over Europe, and, in fact, the world. The Deauville American Film Festival, established in 1975, pulls in the Hollywood crowd.

THE D-DAY LANDING BEACHES

Normandy

FRANCE

On June 6, 1944, some 133,000 Allied ground and airborne troops landed on five beaches in Normandy, France, to liberate Europe from the Nazis during World War II. More than 4,400 of them were killed during the D-Day invasion. Today, the beaches of Utah, Omaha, Gold, Juno, and Sword are tranquil sites of remembrance; each beach has its own unique landscape, from wide, sandy shores to steep cliffs, providing a scenic backdrop for contemplation. Visitors often come to pay tribute at the numerous war memorials and cemeteries nearby.

BINZ	Rügen	GERMANY

Binz, located on Germany's largest island, Rügen, in the Baltic Sea, is one of Germany's most popular beach destinations. Established at the end of the 19th century, the sophisticated resort town is best known for its ornate white villas that draw from Art Nouveau traditions—and its three-mile-long beach and 2.5-mile-long promenade. The long beach is divided into sections to cater to different interests, from a dog-friendly stretch to a nudist one. The area surrounding Binz, including Jasmund National Park, is filled with lush forests and white cliffs, providing scenic walking and biking paths for nature lovers.

	**LANGEOOG BEACH**	Langeoog	GERMANY

The East Frisian island of Langeoog in the North Sea offers a natural paradise for beachgoers. The island is car-free, preserving its tranquil atmosphere and making it perfect for those seeking some peace and quiet. The beaches of Langeoog stretch for more than eight miles, and sections are dotted with colorful beach huts. After spending time sunbathing on the sand, visit the nearby dunes and nature reserves for scenic walking, biking, and horseback-riding trails. The small town here has plenty of lodgings and cafés to keep you entertained during your vacation to this idyllic island.

NAVAGIO BEACH (SHIPWRECK BEACH)	Zakynthos	GREECE

Navagio Beach, also known as Shipwreck Beach, is one of Greece's most photographed beaches—you've probably seen it on social media more than once. Located on the island of Zakynthos, this secluded cove, which is accessible only by boat, is framed by towering limestone cliffs and features crystal-clear turquoise waters. As you might guess from its name, there is a shipwreck here: the *MV Panagiotis* ran aground in 1980 and it now rests in the center of the beach. Because this area is frequently hit by earthquakes, the beach may be closed due to landslides, so keep that in mind when you're planning a visit here.

	ELAFONISI BEACH	Crete	GREECE

A striking pink-sand beach, Elafonisi Beach on the southwestern coast of Crete was once a hidden gem, but the secret is out. During peak season, it's regularly filled with sunbathing visitors enjoying the picturesque sand or the calm, turquoise waters. For a break from the crowds, wade through the shallow lagoon during low tide to the island of Elafonisi, a protected nature reserve known for its rare flora, including the sea daffodil in the summer and *Androcymbium rechingeri* in the winter. The waters here are a favorite spot of loggerhead sea turtles, too, so don't forget your snorkel.

The Ionian island of Kefalonia is home to Myrtos Beach, widely regarded as one of Greece's most beautiful beaches. Nestled between the bases of two mountains, Agia Dynati and Kalon Oros, the beach features striking white pebbles and azure waters surrounded by marble cliffs—and it's a perfect spot for sunset. There are a few facilities here for your comfort, including sunbed and umbrella rentals and a little café with snacks, but they might not always be open, so do come prepared. For more substantial infrastructure, visit the nearby village of Divarata, where there are restaurants and guesthouses.

MYRTOS BEACH	Kefalonia	GREECE

BALOS BEACH | Crete | GREECE

Crete's Balos Beach takes on an irregular, meandering shape that encircles a bright-turquoise lagoon—the beach's shape changes with the tides, though, so you never know what it'll look like until you get there. This warm lagoon is perfect for swimming, thanks to its warm waters, while the pink-tinged sand draws in the sunbathers. The rocky islet of Imeri Gramvousa offers a hike to a scenic overlook to take in the splendor of the beach and its lagoon, and you'll also find the ruins of a Venetian fortress here.

Many visitors flock to Iceland's iconic Reynisfjara Beach, located near the village of Vik on Iceland's southern coast. The black-sand beach is noted for its towering basalt rock formations, from the Reynisdrangar sea stacks just offshore to the hexagonal columns around Hálsanefshellir Cave. The beach's rugged beauty is worthy of a visit, but you need to be very careful here—this is one of the more dangerous sites in Iceland, as it's known for "sneaker waves" that can easily sneak up on you, knock you down, and drag you out. Pay close attention to the signage advising you of the conditions, and never turn your back to the sea.

	**REYNISFJARA BEACH**	Vik	ICELAND

No, you won't find diamonds on Diamond Beach, but you will find sparkling pieces of ice that look like them! The beach is located near the Jökulsárlón Glacier Lagoon in southeastern Iceland, so crystal-clear glacial ice of all shapes and sizes frequently accumulates along the shore. The ice is made all the more spectacular by a backdrop of black sand, making this beach a photographer's dream. Keep in mind that Diamond Beach is just a nickname—its proper name is Breiðamerkursandur, named for the Breiðamerkurjökull glacier from which all that ice originates.

	**DIAMOND BEACH**	Jökulsárlón	ICELAND

The golden sands of Keem Strand on County Mayo's Achill Island attract beach lovers all year round. The secluded beach, nestled in a horseshoe-shaped bay surrounded by dramatic cliffs and rolling green hills, is a summer hotspot for sunbathing and swimming, while in the colder months, it's a popular place for scenic walks. Take the mile-long walk across the cliffs of Benmore towards Achill Head, or make your way across the bay to the deserted village at Slievemore. Keem Strand is also a popular spot for surfing and kayaking.

	KEEM STRAND	Achill Island, County Mayo	IRELAND

SCALA DEI TURCHI	Sicily	ITALY

Sicily's Scala dei Turchi, which means "the Turkish steps," features striated white marl cliffs that do, indeed, look like a staircase. Of course, they're rather steep, so they're not an easy staircase to climb! The cliffs do have beautiful, powdery sand at their base, though—these beaches have formed from the cliffs' erosion over time. To protect this fragile geological feature, it's best visited by boat tour, some of which offer snorkeling excursions in the area. While visiting this part of Sicily, don't miss a visit to the hilltop city of Agrigento, perhaps best known for the ruins of the ancient city of Akragas.

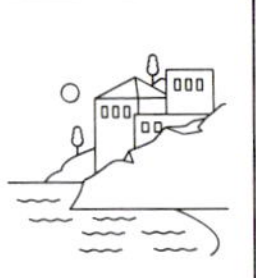

ATRANI BEACH	Campania	ITALY

Today, Atrani might not be as famous as its neighbor Amalfi, but this tiny town—the smallest in Italy at less than five hundredths of a square mile—is just as picturesque. And its crescent-shaped beach is often delightfully uncrowded compared with other Amalfi Coast hotspots. The sandy stretch is family-friendly thanks to its calm waters and ample loungers and umbrellas, and it's the perfect place to spend a day on the seaside. Atrani is just a 15-minute walk from Amalfi, yet it's still something of a hidden gem.

	**LA PELOSA BEACH**	Sardinia	ITALY

Sardinia's La Pelosa Beach is one of the most famous beaches in Italy—it's known for its fine white sand and turquoise seas that are reminiscent of the Caribbean. The beach offers stunning views of the 16th-century La Pelosa Tower that sits on a small islet just offshore. Before 2018, this scenic beach was overrun with visitors during the peak summer season, but now entry to the beach is capped at 1,500 per day (and no longer free) to preserve the natural environment. Beyond this, all visitors must place their beach towels on a straw mat to help keep the sand on the beach.

Located between Camogli and Portofino on the Ligurian coast, the cove of San Fruttuoso can be reached only by sea or a two-hour hike—but it's well worth the journey. While the small pebble beach itself is lovely, its backdrop is perhaps the highlight here: there's a 10th-century abbey that sits right on the shoreline. San Fruttuoso is also home to the underwater statue of *Christ of the Abyss* by artist Guido Galletti, which is a popular diving spot. Its combination of natural beauty and cultural heritage makes it a unique destination along the Italian Riviera.

	SAN FRUTTUOSO	Liguria	ITALY

	WIED IL-GĦASRI	Gozo	MALTA

On Malta's Gozo island, at the very end of the Wied il-Għasri, or Għasri Valley, a teensy pebble beach is sandwiched between two white limestone cliffs, the narrow gorge extending all the way to the sea. This spectacular spot might not have much room for sunbathing, but it's extraordinarily scenic—and it's great for swimming, snorkeling, and scuba diving (there are underwater caves here). To get down to the beach, you'll have to descend a steep staircase cut into the cliff walls. If you swim out to the mouth of the gorge, you might notice a shaft cut into the cliffs—this was once used to hoist buckets of seawater up to fill the nearby salt pans.

	SVETI STEFAN BEACH	Budva	MONTENEGRO

Two crescent-shaped beaches abut a causeway that leads to the fortified islet of Sveti Stefan, located near Budva, Montenegro. While parts of these beaches are private, a large sweep of the pink-pebble beach is open to the public, and it's a popular spot to recline all day long in a sun lounger. The beach has beautiful views of the red-roofed historic buildings on Sveti Stefan, and it's lined with beach bars popular with day-trippers from Budva and hotels for those looking to extend their stay in this picturesque location.

AMELAND	West Frisian Islands	THE NETHERLANDS

Ameland, one of the Dutch Wadden Islands, also known as the Frisian Islands, in the North Sea, is known for its long, sandy beaches lined with rolling dunes. The barrier island's beaches stretch for more than 16 miles, offering plenty of space for swimming, sunbathing, and beachcombing. There are four charming little villages on the island, as well as a beach club for those looking for a hip scene. Ameland is also part of the Wadden Sea UNESCO World Heritage Site and one of the most important areas for migratory birds in the world.

It's hard to believe this white-sand beach is located above the Arctic Circle—its sands are something you might expect to see in tropical latitudes. Uttakleiv Beach, located in the tiny community of Vestvågøy in the Lofoten Islands of Norway, offers a stunning contrast of natural elements, from that powdery white sand to grass-covered (and sometimes snow-covered) cliffs to turquoise waters. Perhaps unsurprisingly, the beach is popular among photographers, particularly for its breathtaking views of the midnight sun in the summer and the Northern Lights in the winter. While the water is very cold here, you might spot surfers braving the cold temperatures.

	UTTAKLEIV BEACH	Vestvågøy	NORWAY

	HAUKLAND BEACH	Vestvågøy	NORWAY

Haukland Beach is one of Uttakleiv's neighbors in Norway's Lofoten Islands. It, too, is one of the country's most picturesque beaches, with white sand, azure seas, and a mountainous backdrop, but it does have a bit more infrastructure here—in the summer, a beach café provides refreshments. There are camping areas here, or you can stay in the nearby town of Leknes. Don your hiking boots and hit the mountain trails in the area, which offer panoramic vistas of the beach and surrounding islands. In the winter months, Haukland Beach becomes a fantastic location for viewing the Northern Lights, adding to its allure year-round.

It takes some effort to get to Praia da Ursa, but it's well worth the journey. Drive about 30 minutes west of Sintra via twisting and turning roads, park your car, then hike another 30 minutes down the cliffs to get to the sand. This secluded beach is surrounded by towering sea stacks that feel as if they could be on another planet—in fact, the beach is named after one that looks like a bear. If you're a bit hot from your hike, take a refreshing dip in the cold Atlantic (but beware the waves and currents here).

	**PRAIA DA URSA**	Cabo da Roca	PORTUGAL

	PRAIA DO CAMILO	Lagos, Algarve	PORTUGAL

Praia do Camilo is certainly not the biggest beach in the Algarve region of Portugal, but it's one of the most beautiful. The small stretch of sand is surrounded by golden cliffs, while calm (and fairly warm) blue-green waters are ideal for swimming, snorkeling, and kayaking. To get there, you'll have to descend some 200 wooden steps from the clifftop—and if you get hungry, you'll have to climb back up, as there's a restaurant at the top. If you don't want to make the descent to the beach, it's worth coming out to the scenic overlook at the top of the cliff to take in the view.

	PRAIA DE BENAGIL	Algarve	PORTUGAL

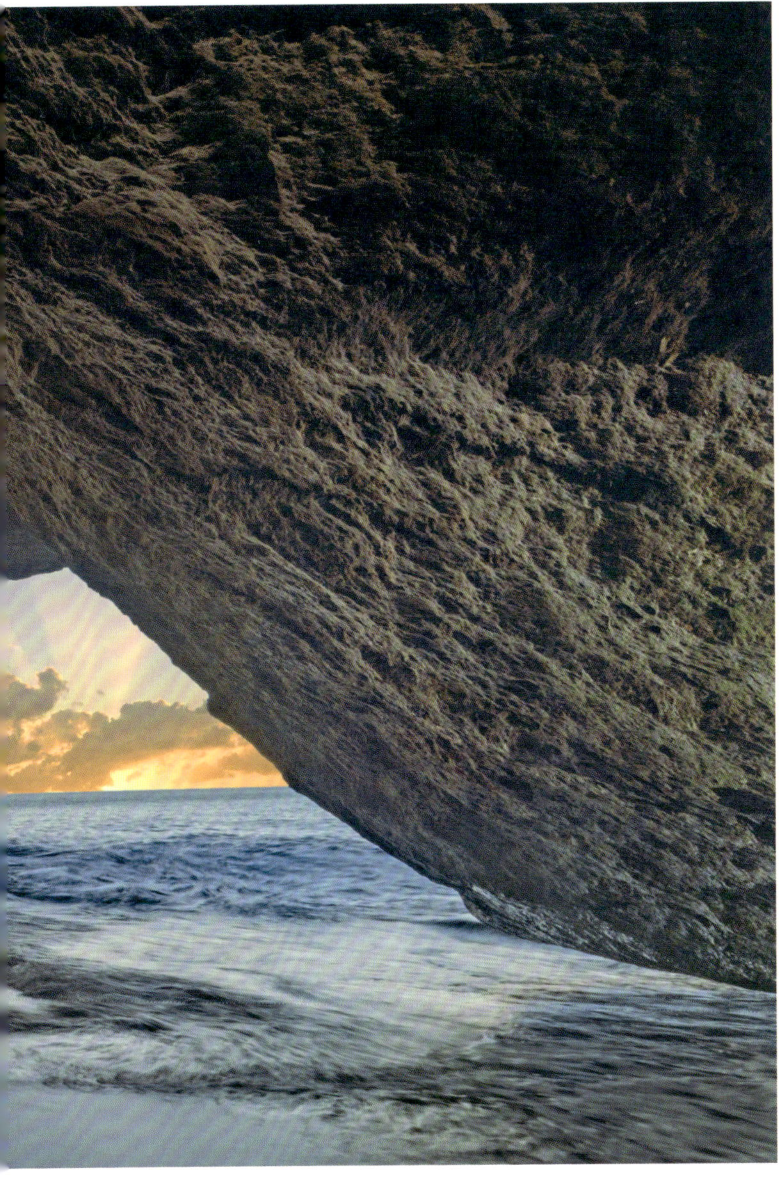

It's less about the beach at Praia de Benagil and more about what's just beyond it: the Benagil Cave. This monumental sea cave has a dome-like shape with a round "skylight" at the top, plus several arches that are open to the ocean. Consider it one of the best natural works of architecture in the world! The Benagil Cave is accessible only by boat, although you can paddle there from the beach if the sea is calm. As you might expect, it can get crowded both in the cave and on the beach.

Cala Macarelleta is one of the most beautiful petite beaches on the island of Menorca, one of Spain's Balearic Islands. To get there, you'll start at Cala Macaralleta's neighbor, Cala Macarella, which is a bigger, family-friendly beach with a restaurant—and it, too, is beautiful. Take the staircase up the cliffs at the end of the beach; then walk about a mile along a rocky trail. You'll eventually emerge at Cala Macarelleta, which has beautiful powdery sand and calm, bright-blue water. The trail is part of a larger network in the region that can make for a beautiful day trip.

	CALA MACARELLETA	Menorca	SPAIN

It may not be truly silent at Playa del Silencio in the Asturias region of Spain, but it's certainly a tranquil place. While the Bay of Biscay can have rough seas, this beach is sheltered and often has calm waters. Here, a narrow stretch of beach is surrounded by lush cliffs, and there are no buildings in sight. See? Peaceful. As with many cliff-lined beaches, there's a descent involved to get to the sand, but there's also a scenic overlook for those who want to take in the view of the rugged landscape and serene beach from the top.

	PLAYA DEL SILENCIO	Asturias	SPAIN

PRAIA DAS CATEDRAIS

Ribadeo, Galicia

SPAIN

Praia das Catedrais, also known as As Catedrais, is a dedicated Natural Monument in Galicia, Spain. It does indeed have cathedral-like natural architecture, all formed by the wind and the sea, of course—at low tide, you can walk beneath towering rock arches as if you're strolling through the nave of a cathedral. But when the tide is high, you'll have to take in the scene from the top of the cliffs, which is a spectacular view in its own right. Access to this beach is free, but you do need a reservation to enter, as the government of Galicia has implemented crowd-control measures to protect the natural landscape here.

Had enough of partying in Ibiza? Retreat to Cala Llentrisca, a quiet cove in the rural southwest of the island with a small pebble beach lined with old fishing huts and surrounded by pine forests. It's quite the juxtaposition from the clubby atmosphere found elsewhere on the island during the summer. To get there, you'll need to take a fairly rocky cliffside trail, so be sure to wear sturdy shoes. And don't forget to bring your snorkel gear to explore the underwater world in the cove!

	CALA LLENTRISCA	Ibiza	SPAIN

This beach might have a foreboding name, and it might require a hike down a slightly treacherous trail to get there, but if you can brave it all safely, you'll be rewarded with a scenic pebble beach with crystal-clear water. Located in Cabo de Gata-Níjar Natural Park in Almería, Playa de los Muertos has a rugged, wild landscape. There are a number of hiking trails in the region—you can hike along the cliffs to reach the Mesa Roldán lighthouse from the beach. As for that aforementioned hike to get to the beach, you have a few options: there's a steep trail, a very steep trail, and a less steep trail with steps. Or you can book a boat trip from Carboneras.

	**PLAYA DE LOS MUERTOS**	Almería	SPAIN

	PLAYA EL MEJILLÓN	Fuerteventura, Canary Islands	SPAIN

Playa El Mejillón, also known as Popcorn Beach, does not have powdery sand. It has, as you might have guessed, popcorn-esque sand. The sand takes this unusual shape thanks to rhodoliths, a type of red algae that forms calcareous nodules resembling coral. And when the strong waves dash the rhodoliths to bits on the shore, the result is popcorn-looking sand. (You might be tempted to take the sand home as a souvenir, but please don't, as removing the sand is strictly forbidden to preserve the beach.) Speaking of the strong waves, this is a hotspot for surfers—expert ones, as the sea is challenging here.

PLATJA GRAN DE TOSSA DE MAR

Costa Brava

SPAIN

Tossa de Mar is a charming beach town located on the Costa Brava in Catalonia, Spain, and it's known for its golden Platja Gran beach, set beneath a fortified hilltop village that overlooks the Mediterranean Sea. Visitors can enjoy swimming, sunbathing, or strolling along the promenade lined with restaurants and shops. While the Platja Gran is a picturesque spot for a beach day, it does tend to get quite crowded during the summer. Fortunately, it's not the only beach in town: Cala Pola and Cala Giverola are nearby coves worthy of a visit.

SANDHAMMAREN	Österlen	SWEDEN

Sandhammaren Beach, located in southern Sweden's Österlen region, is known for its incredibly soft white sand and expansive dunes. Often considered one of the best beaches in the country, Sandhammaren draws in the crowds every summer. But the beach stretches for miles, offering plenty of space for relaxation, long walks, and sunbathing in the nude—there's a naturist area here. If you're more interested in a different kind of nature, just north of the beach is a protected nature reserve ideal for birding—it's also home to Sweden's southernmost elk population.

RHOSSILI BAY BEACH	Gower Peninsula	WALES, UNITED KINGDOM

The three-mile-long stretch of sand near the village of Rhossili on Wales's Gower Peninsula is one of the best beaches in the U.K.—for dogs and dog lovers, specifically. It's dog-friendly year-round, so there's always a good chance you'll spot a four-legged friend or two while you're there. But the beach is a gorgeous spot for a dog-free walk, too, as well as sunbathing and swimming. At low tide, you can walk out to Worm's Head, a tidal island with superb hiking, but make sure you register with the Coastwatch Station first. To get to Rhossili Bay Beach, you'll have to hike a quarter mile down (or up) a steep path.

KYNANCE COVE	Lizard Peninsula, Cornwall	ENGLAND, UNITED KINGDOM

Kynance Cove is a dramatic tidal beach on Cornwall's stunning Lizard Peninsula, which means it's best explored at low tide, when its serpentinite sea stacks, caves, and smaller coves are revealed by the retreating waters. Many features have Victorian-era names, which is appropriate since Queen Victoria and Prince Albert are known to have visited here. The beauty of this wild beach has also drawn in artists, including the poet Alfred Tennyson, to immortalize the beach through their works. Just be wary of the tide, as it's possible you could get cut off by it on your journey across the sand.

VATERSAY

Outer Hebrides

SCOTLAND, UNITED KINGDOM

The remote island of Vatersay in the Scottish Outer Hebrides is lined with sandy beaches and dunes, the most notable of which flank a narrow isthmus. As beautiful as this beachy region is, there has been tragedy here. In 1853, a severe storm sank the Annie Jane, ferrying emigrants from England to Quebec; some 350 men, women, and children died, and they're now honored by a memorial on the beach. Then in 1944, a Royal Air Force Catalina seaplane crashed on the hillside near the beach, killing three crew members; the wreck remains in its final resting place. On a more positive note, Vatersay is home to the start of the 200-mile Hebridean Way walking trail, and it does provide a very scenic send-off.

	ACHMELVICH BEACH	Lochinver	SCOTLAND, UNITED KINGDOM

White sands and turquoise seas? Welcome to Scotland. Sure, the dog-friendly Achmelvich Beach might not be what you'd expect from this northern country, but it's a delight for all who come to visit it. The beach is particularly known as a recreational destination, with activities ranging from waterskiing to windsurfing to kayaking, as well as fishing and birding. And it's surrounded by rugged hills and mountains, including the famous Suilven, making this a paradise for hikers and climbers. Many of these outdoorsy types make the nearby camping and caravan park their home base while they're enjoying the area.

Located on the Lulworth Estate in Dorset, on England's Jurassic Coast, Durdle Door is one of the most famous rock formations in the U.K. This lime natural arch, which juts out from the pebbly Durdle Door Beach, was designated as the first natural UNESCO World Heritage Site in England in 2001. While the beach isn't the best for sunbathing or swimming—it's quite pebbly and the current here is rough—it provides the best view of the Durdle Door. From the beach, you can also hike to the gorgeous Lulworth Cove.

	**DURDLE DOOR BEACH**	Jurassic Coast, Dorset	ENGLAND, UNITED KINGDOM

The vastness of Luskentyre Beach is breathtaking. Located on the Isle of Harris in Scotland's Outer Hebrides, this landscape is filled with grass-covered dunes of soft white sand, rolling hills and mountains, and azure seas. Perhaps unsurprisingly, this is a popular spot for long strolls, as well as more active hikes up the nearby slopes. As the water is cold, you'll find only brave swimmers in it, but there are often kayakers, paddleboarders, kitesurfers, and windsurfers here. The beach is best visited at low tide when you can see just how expansive it is.

	LUSKENTYRE BEACH	Isle of Harris, Outer Hebrides	SCOTLAND, UNITED KINGDOM

If you can read the word *Copacabana* without bursting into song, I'm impressed. But in this book, it's not about the nightclub of which Barry Manilow sings—it's for its namesake, the iconic Copacabana Beach in Rio de Janeiro. Stretching for more than two miles along the city's coast and lined with an instantly recognizable black-and-white wave-patterned pavement, this famous beach is the life of the party. It's always bustling here, with active beach volleyball games to blasting music pouring out of the bars and clubs to the vendors hawking various street foods. Copacabana is also very well known for its New Year's Eve celebrations, when millions flock to the sand to watch a grand fireworks show.

	**COPACABANA**	Rio de Janeiro	BRAZIL

IPANEMA	Rio de Janeiro	BRAZIL

Ipanema in Rio de Janeiro is another world-famous beach, located right next to Copacabana, and it, too, is known for its vibrant atmosphere. (Sunbathing! Beach volleyball! Surfing!) That said, it has a bit more of a chic, upscale atmosphere than its neighbor. Just at the edge of its golden sands is quite the social scene, with numerous bars, cafés, and restaurants lining the streets. The beach is divided into sections, each catering to different crowds, from families to surfers to the LGBTQ+ community, so you can choose which suits you best. While you'll find people here all day long, sunset draws perhaps the biggest crowds to Ipanema, as the views are magnificent.

Praia do Forte is one of Brazil's most beautiful beaches—and that's saying a lot, since this is a country known for its beaches. Unlike the party-centric beaches of Rio de Janeiro, this beach on the Coconut Coast in Bahia is a popular destination for both all-inclusive resorts and wildlife tourism, particularly for whale watching and sea turtle conservation. Humpback whales migrate past the beach between July and October, while sea turtles hatch from September to March. Even if you're not here in hatchling season, you can visit the conservation organization Projeto Tamar, which protects the sea turtles here.

	**PRAIA DO FORTE**	Coconut Coast	BRAZIL

JERICOACOARA BEACH	Ceará	BRAZIL

For a different style of Brazilian beach, make your way to Jericoacoara, or Jeri, for short, in Ceará. Set within Jericoacoara National Park, this beach is known for its natural landscapes, particularly its massive sand dunes and crystal-clear lagoons. It's rather remote, though—it's nearly 200 miles from the closest major city, Fortaleza. But that doesn't stop visitors, in particular, watersports enthusiasts. Jericoacoara Beach has pretty consistent winds, which make it a top kitesurfing and windsurfing destination. Despite its remoteness, there is a lovely little town here with accommodations, restaurants, and bars that make Jericoacoara the perfect vacation destination.

	MARAGOGI BEACH	Alagoas	BRAZIL

South of Recife in Alagoas is Maragogi Beach, known for its gentle, turquoise waters that have earned the region the nickname "the Brazilian Caribbean." In particular, Maragogi is known for the natural pools, or *galés*, that form off the coast during low tide—these natural pools are surrounded by coral, providing excellent snorkeling and scuba-diving opportunities. It almost feels like you're swimming in an aquarium, but this is *real*. Just off Maragogi Beach is the town of Maragogi, where you'll find accommodations and beach bars and restaurants. And while you're here, make the short drive south to Japaratinga Beach during "dry tide"—you can walk out hundreds of feet into the ocean, but the water remains just a foot deep or so.

BAÍA DOS PORCOS	Fernando de Noronha	BRAZIL

Despite its diminutive size—it's about 330 feet long—Baía dos Porcos is absolutely worthy of a visit. You'll find this tiny beach on the eponymous main island of the Fernando de Noronha Archipelago, located more than 200 miles off the coast of mainland Brazil. Thanks to this remote destination's incredible biodiversity, it is both a marine national park and a UNESCO World Heritage Site. Baía dos Porcos is rather difficult to get to, as you'll have to hike there via a steep, rocky trail, but you'll be rewarded with emerald waters (bring a snorkel!) and perfect views of dramatic rock formations, including the Dois Irmãos, or Two Brothers.

	**LEOPARD BEACH**	Falkland Islands	BRITISH OVERSEAS TERRITORY

No, you won't find any leopards on Leopard Beach—but you will find gentoo and Magellanic penguins here. This half-mile stretch of white sand is located on Carcass Island in the Falkland Islands (or, as Argentina calls them, Islas Malvinas), and it's an appealing destination for birders. Besides penguins, songbirds take up residence here, including the endemic Cobb's wren. Leopard Beach will likely have elephant seals and sea lions on shore during your visit, too, so it's not *just* a beach for birders. And there's the fact that the beach itself is simply beautiful to look at, particularly with the bright-blue water, white-sand beach, and green tufts of native tussac.

Chile has some 4,000 miles of coastline, so it should come as little surprise that it has quite the range of beaches. Bahía Inglesa on the edge of the Atacama Desert is one of the most interesting, thanks to the striking contrast between the stark desert landscape and the turquoise sea. The beach's fine white sand and gentle waters make it a popular destination for family vacations, while adventure seekers might enjoy the area's scenic hikes. Off the beach, the village of Bahía Inglesa is known for its seafood restaurants and small guesthouses providing a local experience.

	**BAHÍA INGLESA**	Atacama Desert	CHILE

On the Pacific coast of Colombia, the town of Nuquí has some beautiful beaches, but that's only the start of what this off-the-beaten-path destination has to offer. Paired with these beaches is extraordinary biodiversity of both flora and fauna. In the marine ecosystem, humpback whales are the star of the show; whale-watching season runs from July to November. Then right off the beach is the tropical rainforest, home to birds of paradise, colorful (and sometimes poisonous) frogs, and howler monkeys. And if you're interested in culture, Nuquí is home to one of Colombia's primary Afro-Colombian communities—stay at a guesthouse to learn about the local cultural heritage (and gastronomy!).

	**NUQUÍ**	Chocó	COLOMBIA

SAN ANDRÉS — COLOMBIA

San Andrés is not a beach itself, but rather a seahorse-shaped island in the Caribbean Sea that's one of Colombia's best beach destinations. As such, it draws the crowds—many of its main beaches, such as the family-friendly Cocoplum and high rise-lined Spratt Bight, are anything but under-the-radar. While they're still beautiful beaches worth visiting, if you're looking for a little more space on the sand, head for Playa San Luis, a quieter, more laid-back beach about 5.5 miles outside of the main town of Centro that's noted for its colorful wooden houses.

PLAYA DE LOS FRAILES	Machalilla National Park	ECUADOR

Many beaches vie to win the designation of their country's most beautiful beach. In Ecuador, Playa de Los Frailes is certainly in the running. Located within Machalilla National Park, this crescent-shaped gray-sand beach is surrounded by cliffs on either end; on one side, you can hike up to a *mirador*, or scenic overlook. Since this beach is in a protected area, there are no commercial establishments on the beach itself, making it an ideal destination for those who appreciate a more natural setting. But there still is a bit of infrastructure here—off the parking lot are bathrooms with showers and a concession stand.

The Galápagos Islands are certainly more of a wildlife destination than a sunbathing destination, but that doesn't mean there's a shortage of picturesque beaches here. You'll just have to share them with animals! Tortuga Bay, located on the island of Santa Cruz, is walkable from the main town of Puerto Ayora, and it's home to two white-sand beaches: Playa Brava and Playa Mansa. The former has a stronger current, so it's best to stay on the sand here, while the latter is much calmer and ideal for swimming and kayaking. Across both beaches, you'll likely spot marine iguanas, finches, blue-footed boobies, and sea lions. And if you go snorkeling, you might come upon white-tip reef sharks.

	TORTUGA BAY	Santa Cruz, Galápagos	ECUADOR

	BARTOLOMÉ ISLAND BEACH	Bartolomé Island, Galápagos	ECUADOR

Bartolomé Island in the Galápagos might be only half a square mile in size, but it fits a lot into that little footprint. Before you hit the beach here, climb to the summit of the old volcano and take in the panoramic views from the top—this is perhaps one of the most photographed locations in the whole archipelago. And you'll certainly work up a sweat when you do, which makes snorkeling in the cool waters off the beach all the more enjoyable. The beach itself has perfect views of the striking Pinnacle Rock, but the best view might just be underwater; here you might spot Galápagos penguins, colorful sea stars, and even a white-tip reef shark or two.

Machu Picchu might get the lion's share of the attention in Peru, but don't forget that this is a coastal country—and that means there are beaches. Máncora is perhaps the best-known beach destination in Peru, with a bit of a reputation as a party town. While the town and its adjacent beach are, quite frankly, a little chaotic, you can hop in a *tuk tuk* to find more peaceful locations. Just three miles outside of town are Las Pocitas tidal pools that are great for beach walking, while a bit farther is Playa Vichayito, a watersports haven. Keep an eye out for migrating humpback whales between the months of July and October!

	**MÁNCORA**	Piura	PERU

Pilsen

PLAYA ROJA	Paracas National Reserve	PERU

There are no surprises when it comes to Playa Roja, thanks to its very literal name. Red Beach, as it'd be called in English, does indeed have red sand, formed by the ocean's erosion of the volcanic pink granodiorite rock here. Those reddish grains create a striking contrast to the ochre cliffs behind them and the deep-azure sea in front of them. Playa Roja is set within the Paracas National Reserve, and while swimming isn't advisable due to the rough seas, the beach is perfect for photography and birdwatching, as the area is home to many species of seabirds.

PUNTA DEL ESTE — URUGUAY

If you're looking for a glamorous resort town in Uruguay, Punta del Este is it. Luxury hotels, over-the-top nightclubs, and 20 miles of beaches on Uruguay's Atlantic coast define this vacation destination, and they attract tourists from all over the world, particularly during the summer months when the beach clubs, restaurants, and bars come to life. There are two main beaches in town, Playa Mansa, which has calmer seas, and Playa Brava, which has stronger seas. Playa Brava is also home to the famous "hand in the sand" sculpture, formally called *La Mano*, by Chilean artist Mario Irarrázabal; it has a twin in Chile's Atacama Desert.

	**PUNTA DEL DIABLO**	—	URUGUAY

Despite its name, Punta del Diablo is far more charming than it is devilish. In fact, it's the counterpoint to Punta del Este, with a far more peaceful atmosphere and more quaint accommodations—there are more surfers and backpackers here than nightclubbers and see-and-be-seen-ers. That said, this beach destination does get crowded in the high season, which runs from December through March. Playa del Rivero is the main beach in town, but a 20-minute walk brings you to Playa Grande within Santa Teresa National Park—there's a great whale-watching point in this serene place.

From above, the island of Cayo de Agua in Venezuela's Los Roques Archipelago National Park looks like an abstract oil painting, with various blues and beiges dancing around each other in large swirls. What you're really seeing, though, is two islands connected by a long sandbar, plus coral reefs beneath the sea. It's accessible only by boat from Gran Roque, so you'll need to book a ride over to enjoy its stunning white sand and warm, clear waters. Pack everything you need for the day, from food to towels to snorkel gear—there are no amenities on this little island!

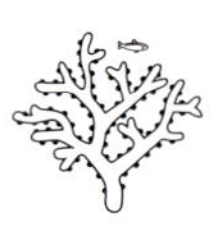	CAYO DE AGUA	Los Roques Archipelago National Park	VENEZUELA

CARLISLE BAY BEACH	Old Road, Antigua	ANTIGUA AND BARBUDA

Southern Antigua's Carlisle Bay, a natural crescent-shaped harbor, is your picture-perfect Caribbean beach: a thin crescent of fine golden sand curves around the turquoise sea, behind which you'll find rainforest-covered hills. Most of the beach is occupied by the Carlisle Bay Resort, which has accommodations overlooking the sand, but there's also a not-too-crowded public access point on the other end of the beach by the town of Old Road. Bring a snorkel mask and fins to see all sorts of tropical fish in the bay.

Aruba's Eagle Beach is the country's widest, boasting plenty of soft white sand to accommodate many visitors without feeling too crowded. It has two signature draws. First, there's a highly photographed pair of fofoti trees on the beach; their gnarled trunks make them particularly sculptural. And second, this is a sea turtle nesting hotspot. Of course, both the trees and the turtles are protected by law, but you can still take pictures of them. There are a handful of low-rise hotels behind the beach; for resorts, head just south to Manchebo Beach, which is the westernmost point in Aruba, as well as Divi Beach.

	**EAGLE BEACH**	Oranjestad	ARUBA

Fortunately Aruba's Flamingo Beach does not mislead you with its name—flamingos do live here, and they're quite the photo op. But the beach itself is a lovely spot to spend a few hours, whether you book a private cabana or grab a seat at Mangrove Beach Bar & Fish Shack. Now here's the important bit: the beach is on the private Renaissance Island, and only adult guests of the Renaissance Wind Creek Aruba Resort can visit. But you're not totally out of luck if you're not a Renaissance guest—there are day passes available, but they sell out quickly. For families, there's the neighboring Iguana Beach, which does have iguanas.

	**FLAMINGO BEACH**	Renaissance Island	ARUBA

	PINK SANDS BEACH	Harbour Island	BAHAMAS

For some three miles along Harbour Island, pale-pink sand runs along the shoreline. The appropriately named Pink Sands Beach gets its hue from the crushed reddish-pink shells of microscopic organisms known as foraminifera.
If you're looking for the perfect photograph, know that the pinkest part of the beach is right along the waterline, where the sand is wet. But put down the camera and spend some time enjoying this beach, too. The water is warm year-round here, so it's great for swimming and snorkeling. And the pink sand has a special feature besides its hue—it stays cool even in the midday sun, so you won't burn your feet during a long walk on the beach.

	BROWNES BEACH	Bridgetown	BARBADOS

The most beautiful beaches in the Caribbean aren't all secluded, far-flung spots. Brownes Beach in Bridgetown, Barbados, is one of the country's best beaches, and it's right in the heart of town. Because of its easy-to-access location, Brownes Beach does often have crowds on its white sand. But there is a silver lining here—that popularity means there are a number of watersports vendors on the beach, as well as beach clubs from which you can rent umbrellas and loungers. And definitely make time for a snorkeling or scuba-diving excursion here, as there are six shipwrecks in the bay that are now home to plenty of sea life.

Horseshoe Bay has it all—pink sand, limestone cliffs, and cool blue waters. *And* it's free to access, though that means that it can get crowded. As Horseshoe Bay is a rather protected beach, the swimming and snorkeling are excellent here. If you want an even more protected area for kids, visit the beach's Port Royal Cove, which has shallow water and virtually no waves. Off the beach, you'll find walking trails through the dunes—you can even take one to the neighboring Warwick Long Bay.

	HORSESHOE BAY	Southampton Parish	BERMUDA

PINK BEACH — BONAIRE

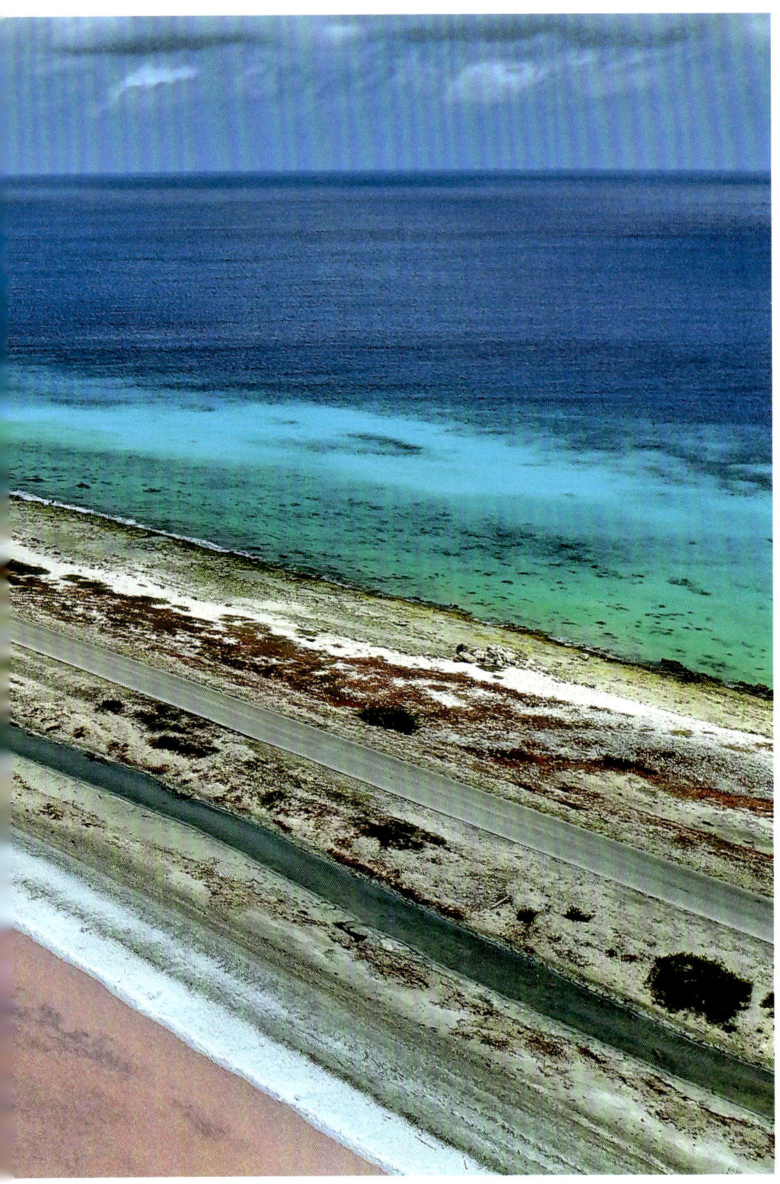

As with many pink-sand beaches, the tinge of pink in the sand at Pink Beach along Bonaire's southern coast comes from the crushed-up shells of foraminifera, a simple microscopic marine organism. But interestingly, most people don't come here for the sand—they come here for the coral reefs. The beach is a favorite among snorkelers and divers looking to experience all the marine life just offshore, and the clear, calm waters provide the perfect conditions to do so. While the beach itself is quite narrow, it's a good spot to haul out after a snorkeling stint and maybe even take a little nap in the sun.

	THE BATHS	Virgin Gorda	BRITISH VIRGIN ISLANDS

Virgin Gorda, the third-largest island of the British Virgin Islands, was named by Christopher Columbus for its profile view, which looks like a reclining woman. Its most famous attraction is, undoubtedly, the Baths, a beach covered in massive granite boulders, remnants of a long-ago volcanic eruption worn smooth by the wind and waves. The boulders create natural caves and grottoes filled with sand and occasionally filled by the rising tide—it's a delight to scramble through them, taking a dip in the tidal pools that form here. If there's any downside to the Baths, it's that they often get crowded, especially when cruise ships are in port. For more breathing room, visit the Baths at dawn or in the late afternoon.

SAN JOSEF BAY

Vancouver Island,
British Columbia

CANADA

Don a pair of hiking shoes and head off on a 45-minute trek through Vancouver Island's Cape Scott Provincial Park to find this remote beach. With powdery sand, jagged sea stacks, and hidden sea caves to explore, this beach has plenty to keep adventure seekers entertained. At low tide, you can walk around the sea stacks and caves, but keep an eye on the water—at high tide, you'll need a kayak or paddleboard to access these areas. If you'd like to spend more than a day here, you can tent camp here for a small fee.

	**LAKE ANNETTE**	Jasper National Park, Alberta	CANADA

The Canadian Rockies might not be *best* known for their beaches, but perhaps they should be. Lake Annette, located in Jasper National Park in Alberta, is a stunning alpine lake surrounded by forested mountains—and it has a beach. This is a popular spot for travelers looking to relax a bit on their national park trip; you'll find them picnicking here, playing frisbee, or walking the trail around the lake. If you're feeling brave, you can take a dip in the crystal-clear but cold water. Too chilly for you? Launch a kayak or paddleboard from the dock at the beach.

	SEVEN MILE BEACH	Grand Cayman	CAYMAN ISLANDS

The most famous beach in the Cayman Islands, Seven Mile Beach on Grand Cayman stretches from the outskirts of George Town all the way up to West Bay—though the distance is shy of seven miles. This beach is where you'll find many of the luxury resorts on the island, but the beach is public and you can walk its entire length if you so choose. Seven Mile Beach is known for its calm conditions, making it ideal for swimming, kayaking, and paddleboarding. And with a number of reefs offshore, it's an ideal spot for snorkeling, too.

Manuel Antonio Beach, located within Manuel Antonio National Park on Costa Rica's Pacific coast, is one of the country's most beautiful beaches. Surrounded by lush tropical rainforests, the beach offers white sand and clear blue waters. Other top beaches in the national park include Espadilla Sur and Puerto Escondido; you can travel between each via a series of hiking trails, many of which have scenic overlooks throughout. Be on the sharp lookout for wildlife here, as the national park is home to capuchin monkeys, sloths, coatis, and iguanas, to name a few local residents. Within Manuel Antonio National Park, you'll have an unforgettable beach experience in a very biodiverse part of Costa Rica.

MANUEL ANTONIO BEACH

Manuel Antonio National Park

COSTA RICA

TAMARINDO BEACH

Guanacaste

COSTA RICA

Named for the tamarind trees along its shoreline, Tamarindo Beach on Costa Rica's Pacific coast is one of the country's top surf hubs. It lures surfers and other visitors not only with its waves, but also with its laid-back town filled with beach bars—there's a substantial nightlife scene here. Land-based adventure opportunities abound, too, as Tamarindo provides easy access to Las Baulas National Marine Park, where you'll find even more beaches, plus hiking and horseback-riding trails through the rainforest, not to mention all sorts of flora and fauna. The park is particularly known for its sea turtles.

	**PLAYA CONCHAL**	Guanacaste	COSTA RICA

For a less busy version of Tamarindo, take a 30-minute drive north to Playa Conchal. This is less of a surf beach and more of a swimming and sunbathing beach—come here to kick back and relax, taking in the gentle sounds of the sea and the breeze blowing through the trees. Because the waters are quite calm here, Playa Conchal also has good snorkeling. Whereas many accommodations in Tamarindo are smaller hotels or vacation rentals, this beach has several luxury resorts along its crushed-shell sands, so it's easy to spend a few peaceful days here.

SAONA ISLAND	Cotubanamá National Park	DOMINICAN REPUBLIC

Of Cotubanamá National Park's 162 square miles, 41 of them comprise Saona Island, or Isla Saona, renowned for its gorgeous sand beaches and lively coral reefs. The national park as a whole is one of the most biodiverse areas in the Dominican Republic, with more than 500 species of flora and 300 species of birds—you'll want to bring your binoculars here. Saona Island is accessible only by boat, and you can stay here only for a day trip. But tours frequently depart Punta Cana for Cotubanamá and Saona Island, making it fairly easy to access.

Grenada's sister island Carriacou is home to the beautiful Paradise Beach, located in the village of L'Esterre. This delightfully uncrowded beach is where locals gather on weekends, bringing along food, drink, and good music. Along the waterfront are beach restaurants and bars that welcome visitors with open arms—order an ice-cold beer and listen to some live music. Viewable from the beach is the nearby Sandy Island, a tiny sliver of land known for its long beach. You can take a five-minute boat ride to the island from Paradise Beach.

	PARADISE BEACH	Carriacou	GRENADA

GRAND ANSE BEACH	South Coast	GRENADA

Located just a six-minute drive from Grenada's Maurice Bishop International Airport, Grand Anse Beach is practically waiting for you as you step off the plane. This two-mile stretch of white sand and turquoise sea is perhaps the most famous in Grenada. Grand Anse Beach is lined with hotels, restaurants, bars, and even a spice market—Grenada is known as the Spice Island, after all—providing all the amenities visitors need for a relaxing beach vacation. The beach is also just six miles from the capital city of Saint George's, making for convenient sightseeing.

FRENCHMAN'S COVE	Port Antonio	JAMAICA

Frenchman's Cove is a fairly small beach, just about 300 feet long, but what it lacks in size it makes up for in beauty. The relatively secluded and often uncrowded beach is tucked into a serene cove surrounded by rainforest. Behind the beach, a calm river trickles into the sea; there's a rope swing here that's popular with those seeking the perfect vacation photo. There is a laid-back resort here, as well as a beach shack serving up cold drinks and fresh eats, making it a perfect getaway spot.

	**PLAYA PARAÍSO**	Tulum, Quintana Roo	MEXICO

The Riviera Maya has many picture-perfect beaches, but one of the best in the region is Playa Paraíso in Tulum. Yes, it has all the hallmarks of a beautiful Caribbean beach: white sand, azure waters, palm trees. But it also has restaurants, bars, and beach clubs; accommodations that range from glampsites to boutique hotels; and watersports rentals. The beach is conveniently located to various cenotes and the Tulum Archaeological Site, so it's also a popular spot on day-trip tours of the region.

PLAYA DEL AMOR	Cabo San Lucas, Baja California Sur	MEXICO

Playa del Amor, or Lovers Beach, is a secluded cove sandwiched between craggy rock towers in Cabo San Lucas, Mexico—it's adjacent to the iconic El Arco rock formation that's become something of a symbol of the region. The beach stretches across the Land's End, so you can pick between the calmer, swimmable Sea of Cortez side or the dramatically rough Pacific Ocean side of the beach (jokingly referred to as Divorce Beach by some). To get here, you'll need a boat. Water taxis can be hired from Medano Beach, although if you're adventurous and skilled enough, you can actually paddle yourself there in a kayak.

Take a 15-minute ferry ride from Cancún's bustling Hotel Zone to the vibrant beach destination of Isla Mujeres, known for its colorful buildings and white-sand beaches. Playa Norte is the most famous beach on the island, and it's lined with beach clubs to serve you all day long. Come nightfall, the party moves just off the beach to Avenida Hidalgo. If you're looking for a quieter beach, hop on a golf cart and drive south. You'll also find good snorkeling on this side of the island; Garrafon Park has a lovely reef off its beach.

	**PLAYA NORTE**	Isla Mujeres, Quintana Roo	MEXICO

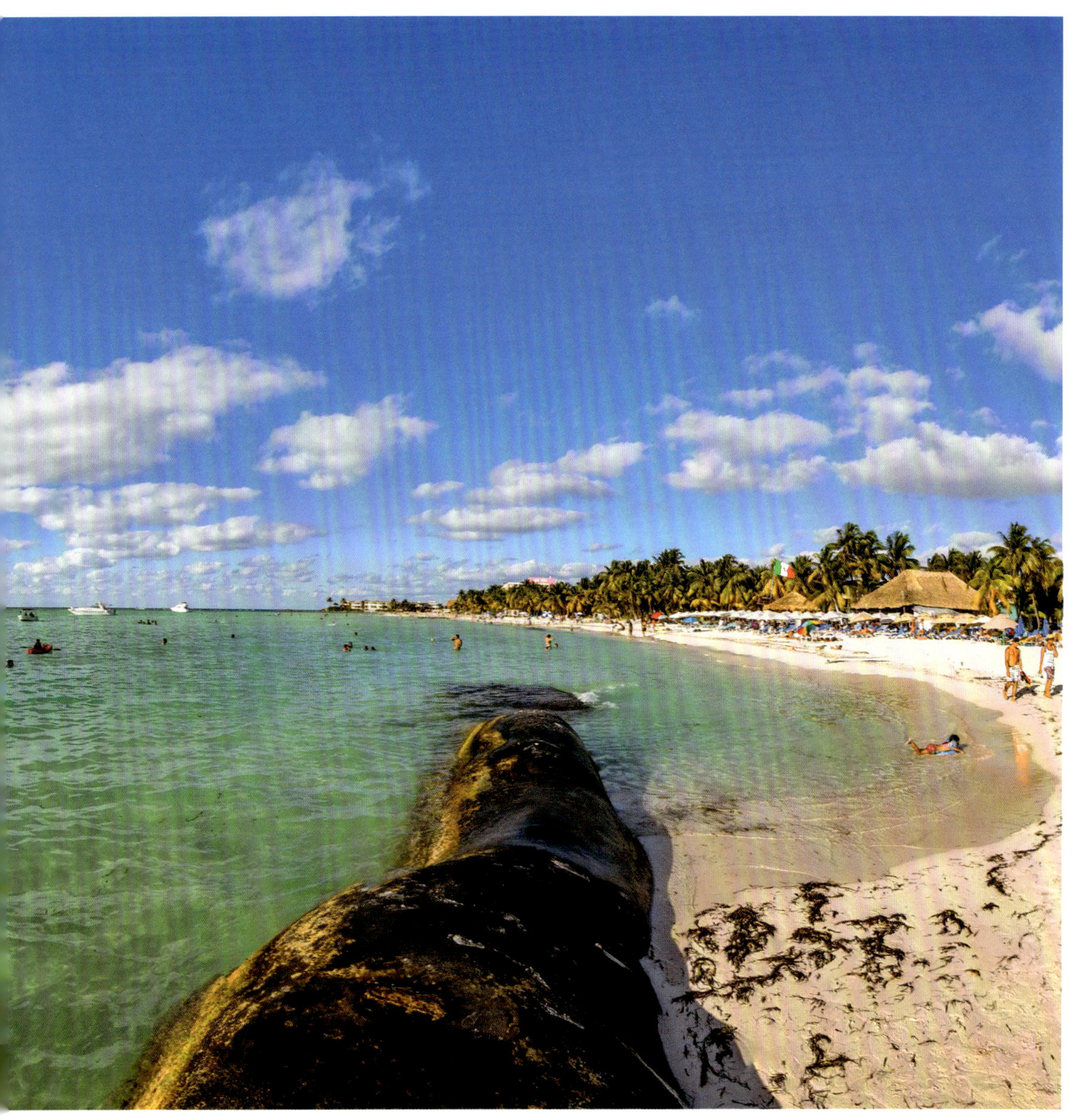

Isla Holbox is the perfect foil to Isla Mujeres. This car-free paradise is delightfully more laid-back, though by no means desolate—there are plenty of bars, restaurants, and boutique accommodations in the Centro district. But the farther out you get from town, the quieter the white-sand beaches get. If you're a wildlife lover, this is also a prime place to go. Between mid-May and mid-September, whale sharks migrate through the waters here—book a tour to go snorkeling with these gentle giants. And just a 30-minute boat ride away is Isla Pajaros, or Bird Island, where you can see dozens of bird species.

ISLA HOLBOX	Quintana Roo	MEXICO

The long beach along South Friar's Bay on the Caribbean side of Saint Kitts is a picturesque beach with calm, clear waters and soft golden sand. While it's a beautiful spot for swimming and sunbathing, it's especially popular due to its lineup of beach bars, clubs, and grills—some of the bigger spots get a little crowded when cruise ships are in port, but there are plenty of locally owned watering holes between them with more elbow room. Off the beach, you'll find hiking trails through the rainforest.

	**SOUTH FRIAR'S BAY**	Saint Kitts	SAINT KITTS AND NEVIS

SUGAR BEACH	Soufrière	SAINT LUCIA

Sugar Beach, formerly known as Jalousie Plantation Beach, is nestled between Saint Lucia's iconic Pitons—two looming volcanic spires that create a breathtaking backdrop. Accessing this beach is an interesting endeavor. The luxurious Sugar Beach, A Viceroy Resort, is located here, so there are amenities reserved for guests only. But it's *also* a public beach. The resort will charge you a fee to take the shuttle down the volcanic cliffs to the sand, but you can walk the path on your own for free, or you can book a water taxi to the beach from elsewhere on the island. Finally, one word to the wise: The sugar white sand is imported. The natural sand in this part of Saint Lucia is grayish-black due to the volcanic activity here.

Anse Chastanet is the name of both a 600-acre luxury resort in Saint Lucia and one of the beaches it sits on. But as with all beaches on the island, part of it is open to the public—you can either park at the resort or take a water taxi directly to the sand. Anse Chastanet is especially known for its snorkeling and diving, but many also come simply to sunbathe. You can also take a walking path from Anse Chastanet to Anse Mamin, another spectacular beach that's technically part of the resort, but also open to the public. Do me a favor and get a burger at the Jungle Beach Bar & Grill on Anse Mamin.

	ANSE CHASTANET	Soufrière	SAINT LUCIA

MAHO BEACH

Maho

SINT MAARTEN

Maho Beach on the Dutch side of Sint Maarten is another one of those beaches where the beach itself isn't the main attraction. This beach is world-famous for its close proximity to the Princess Juliana International Airport. It's located at the very end of the runway, which means that you can watch planes fly directly overhead as they land—or be blasted by jet engines as planes take off. If you visit this beach, please do so carefully, as those jet blasts are no joke! If you move just to the right or left of the runway, though, you'll still get excellent views of the planes without being blown off your feet.

GRACE BAY BEACH	Providenciales	TURKS AND CAICOS

It's hard to overstate the pristine beauty of Grace Bay Beach on the island of Providenciales in Turks and Caicos. This is your quintessential Caribbean beach with white sand and the brightest blue water—and hardly any seaweed, rocks, or pollution, as it's located within the protected Princess Alexandra National Park. The sea here is usually perfectly calm, thanks to (snorkelable!) offshore reefs that protect the bay, and that means it's ideal for all manner of watersports. Taking advantage of this scenic location, luxury resorts, restaurants, and bars can be found up and down the beach.

	FLAMENCO BEACH	Culebra, Puerto Rico	UNITED STATES OF AMERICA

The horseshoe-shaped Flamenco Beach runs for a mile along the coastline of Culebra, one of Puerto Rico's smaller islands. Its name means "flamingo" in Spanish, and it refers to the birds that take up winter residence in a nearby lagoon. This beach is part of the Culebra National Wildlife Refuge, ensuring its natural beauty remains protected—but that wasn't always the case. The beach has two rusting military tanks on its shores, each covered in graffiti. These tanks are reminders of the United States Navy's occupation of the island after World War II.

	MCWAY FALLS	Big Sur, California	UNITED STATES OF AMERICA

Big Sur might just be one of the most scenic coastal destinations in California, a state that has 840 miles of coastline. And at Julia Pfeiffer Burns State Park, you'll find one of the most scenic beaches. For starters, there are the dramatic cliffs behind the golden-sand beach, which are beautiful alone. But then there's McWay Falls, an 80-foot waterfall that cascades down those cliffs directly into the ocean at high tide and onto the beach at low tide. While you can't go down to the beach, you can get a great view from scenic overlooks along a hiking trail at the top of the cliffs.

Arguably one of the most famous beaches in the world, Waikiki Beach in Honolulu, Hawaii, is known for its golden sand, gentle surf, and views of Diamond Head. As such a popular beach, it certainly isn't quiet here. Thousands of visitors flock to this two-mile-long beach every day—some four million people a year—many of whom are staying in one of the hotels that line it. It's a great beach for beginner surf lessons, or for those who want to take a break from the beach for some shave ice, hula pie, or pink snowballs, all of which can be found at the eateries nearby.

	WAIKIKI BEACH	Honolulu, Oahu, Hawaii	UNITED STATES OF AMERICA

DRIFTWOOD BEACH	Jekyll Island, Georgia	UNITED STATES OF AMERICA

Here we have one of the more literally named beaches: Driftwood Beach on Georgia's Jekyll Island. Across this beach are dozens of gnarled, weathered trees that create a surreal landscape. Ultimately, this is a tree graveyard. Most of the trees came from various parts of Jekyll Island that have eroded over the centuries, causing pines and oaks to be lost to the sea. They've washed back ashore, stripped of their leaves and rough bark. While the origin story is a bit grim, Driftwood Beach really is a sight to behold.

Lanikai Beach, also known as Ka'ōhao Beach, provides an entirely different beach experience from Waikiki. Located in Kailua, this tranquil beach offers stunning views of the Mokulua Islands, or "the Mokes," which sit just offshore, making it a popular spot for photography and sunrise viewing. While the area surrounding Lanikai is residential, the beach has public access trails—and it can be busy on the weekends. Visit on a weekday for the smallest crowds. And when you come, be sure to park appropriately—the fines for illegal parking are high to keep the area under control for residents.

	LANIKAI BEACH	Kailua, Oahu, Hawaii	UNITED STATES OF AMERICA

	**CANNON BEACH**	Oregon	UNITED STATES OF AMERICA

The moody, misty coast of Oregon is home to the iconic Cannon Beach. This long, flat beach is best known for Haystack Rock, a 235-foot monolith that rises dramatically from the ocean. As the tide goes out, you can explore the tidal pools at its base, looking for sea stars, green anemones, crabs, and even nudibranchs, or colorful sea slugs. Off the beach, the town of Cannon Beach is a popular destination for art galleries, boutiques, and restaurants. And if you want to explore more of coastal Oregon, I recommend driving five miles south to Hug Point State Recreation Site to see its lovely sandy cove and a seasonal waterfall.

It might not have the most original name, but Sand Beach in Maine's Acadia National Park is worth a visit nonetheless. The beach is—you guessed it—sandy, comprising mostly ground-up shells rather than rocks, making it fairly unique. It's a family-friendly beach within Acadia National Park, and most visitors come to sunbathe rather than swim, as the water rarely breaches 55 degrees Fahrenheit. That said, a swim might be refreshing after you hike the nearby trails, including the popular Beehive, Great Head, and Ocean Path trails.

	**SAND BEACH**	Acadia National Park, Maine	UNITED STATES OF AMERICA

Officially called Kauapea Beach, but better known as Secret Beach, this is probably Hawaii's worst-kept secret. The mile-long, golden-sand beach on the north shore of Kauai is well known, but it's still quite secluded and difficult to reach. First, there are no signs for it. And second, it's accessible only by a steep unmarked trail. So there are still *some* mysteries at Secret Beach—but you can easily find the answers with a little bit of research. If you do make it down to the beach, you're rewarded with beautiful views of the Kīlauea Lighthouse.

KAUAPEA BEACH	Kauai, Hawaii	UNITED STATES OF AMERICA

Dry Tortugas National Park in the Florida Keys is one of the lesser-visited national parks of the United States, but for those willing to make the journey, a pretty special experience awaits. The park is located 70 miles west of Key West, and it's accessible only by boat or seaplane. And most of it is underwater—there are just seven small islands in the 100-square-mile park. While the most famous landside attraction is Fort Jefferson, the largest brick masonry structure in the Americas, there are also beaches here. And beyond the beaches, fantastic snorkeling awaits.

DRY TORTUGAS NATIONAL PARK

Florida Keys, Florida

UNITED STATES OF AMERICA

GLASS BEACH	Fort Bragg, California	UNITED STATES OF AMERICA

Glass Beach in Fort Bragg, California, is just one of three such "glass beaches" in the area. The name comes from the thousands of pieces of sea glass that have washed ashore here, creating a bejeweled beach. The result might be beautiful, but the origin story isn't so nice—the reason so much sea glass accumulated in this area is that locals used to dump their garbage, including glass, into the ocean. Though that practice is now banned, Mother Nature has brought back some of that garbage in the form of smooth sea glass. Before expecting to see an entire beach made of sea glass during your visit, be aware that decades of people collecting the sea glass have greatly diminished the quantity on the beach. Still, it's fun to poke around the beach to spot some of the beauties.

KAIHALULU BEACH	Hana, Maui, Hawaii	UNITED STATES OF AMERICA

Kaihalulu Beach in Hana is also known as Red Sand Beach—can you guess the reason? Yes, the sand is an earthy red here, as it comes from the erosion of a nearby volcanic cinder cone that's rich in iron. The reds contrast spectacularly with the deep-blue water, made all the more beautiful by the green vegetation and the red cliffs. But speaking of those cliffs, please heed this warning: The trail down to the beach is very dangerous, so it should be taken only by highly experienced hikers in good weather conditions.

The beaches throughout all of South Florida have golden sands and aquamarine waters, but there's perhaps no beach in the region as famous as South Beach. Located on the barrier island of Miami Beach, South Beach runs from South Pointe Park to 23rd Street. It's most famous for two things: Art Deco architecture and people watching. As for the architecture, hundreds of colorful buildings popped up here from the 1920s to the 1940s, and the entire Art Deco Historic District became the first 20th-century neighborhood to be recognized by the National Register of Historic Places. As for the people watching, well, you'll see all types here; some are drawn to the muscle beach, some are drawn to the shopping, and some are drawn to the nightlife.

	SOUTH BEACH	Miami Beach, Florida	UNITED STATES OF AMERICA

	**HANALEI BAY**	Kauai, Hawaii	UNITED STATES OF AMERICA

The two-mile-long Hanalei Bay on Kauai's north shore is ringed with gold-sand beaches that are beloved by locals and visitors alike. It's not only the beach that's special—it's the entire area. Behind the beach are lush volcanic peaks, including the famous Bali Hai, that create a dramatic setting. Then there's the rural town of Hanalei, known for its taro fields; the historic Wai'oli Hui'ia Church; and very tasty taro donuts at Holey Grail Donuts. Visit Hanalei and you'll want to stay a while.

The southernmost beach destination in New Jersey, Cape May is a Victorian-era resort town filled with historic gingerbread-style buildings, good eats, and beaches—plenty of them. The main town is flanked by boardwalk-lined beaches dotted with colorful umbrellas throughout the summer. For less-crowded beaches, head west. In Cape May Point State Park, the beach abuts a wildlife refuge that's a hotspot for migrating birds—and it's home to the Cape May Lighthouse and an abandoned World War II–era bunker. Even farther west is Sunset Beach, a west-facing beach where you can see the shipwreck of the *SS Atlantus*, a concrete ship launched in 1918.

	**CAPE MAY**	New Jersey	UNITED STATES OF AMERICA

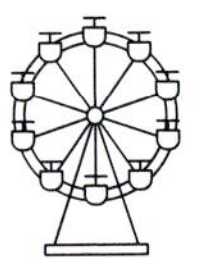

OLD ORCHARD BEACH	Maine	UNITED STATES OF AMERICA

Old Orchard Beach in Maine is a classic New England beach town with a seven-mile stretch of sandy shoreline. For more than 170 years, Mainers and visitors from afar have made this their charming summer home, and you can feel the history everywhere you go. The iconic Old Orchard Beach Pier—Frank Sinatra once sang on the original pier before its demise from storms—is now home to restaurants, shops, and amusement rides, adding to the family-friendly vibe of the town. And this is Maine, so there are plenty of coastal and inland hikes in the area to stretch your legs.

HĀ'ENA BEACH

Island of Hawaii, Hawaii

UNITED STATES OF AMERICA

Hā'ena Beach, also known as Shipman Beach, is a remote spot on the Big Island of Hawaii—to get to this beach, you'll have to hike roughly five miles round-trip along the Puna Historic Trail. It's a fairly strenuous journey, but it's a worthwhile one to see the black and white sands of the secluded beach. Lava rocks form a breakwater a few hundred feet offshore, so the water off the beach is a fairly shallow, calm area for swimming and snorkeling; the water here is brackish, as a freshwater stream runs into the ocean at the beach.

COROLLA

Outer Banks, North Carolina

UNITED STATES OF AMERICA

There are more than 100 miles of beaches in the Outer Banks, a series of barrier islands off the coast of North Carolina. And while pretty much every single one of them is beautiful in its own right, the beaches of Corolla have a bit of an edge over the others—they have wild horses. The horses were originally brought to the island in the 1500s by the Spanish, and today they live free in Corolla and Currituck Counties. While you should always keep your distance from the wild horses, you can take guided tours to see them in their natural habitat on the beach.

ROBERT H. MEYER MEMORIAL STATE BEACH

Malibu, California

UNITED STATES OF AMERICA

The Robert H. Meyer Memorial State Beach comprises a trio of so-called "pocket" beaches: El Matador, La Piedra, and El Pescador. El Matador is best known for its rock formations and sea caves—this is the most crowded of the three. At low tide, you can walk all the way to La Piedra, a less-crowded beach with tide pools and reasonably good surf. There's also a kelp bed just offshore that's popular with both divers and marine mammals. Further west, you'll encounter El Pescador State Beach, which has the longest stretch of sand, bounded by two rocky areas with tide pools. To reach all three beaches, you'll have to park atop the bluffs and descend a series of wooden staircases—it's a bit of a climb, but that's part of the fun.

The Big Island of Hawaii is a hotspot of both active volcanoes and black-sand beaches, and the two are inextricably linked. Black sand is often formed by the erosion of basalt, a volcanic rock. And since there are six major volcanoes on the Big Island, it should come as little surprise that there are many black-sand beaches here. Punalu'u Beach is one of the best known, thanks in part to its sea turtle population. Just leave the swimming here to those sea turtles—the water can be quite rough.

	PUNALU'U BEACH	Ka'ū Coast, Island of Hawaii, Hawaii	UNITED STATES OF AMERICA

JOCKEY'S RIDGE STATE PARK

Outer Banks, North Carolina

UNITED STATES OF AMERICA

At Jockey's Ridge State Park in the Outer Banks of North Carolina, you'll find the tallest living sand dune system on the East Coast. Averaging 80 to 100 feet high, these dunes are "living" in the sense that they're always changing, depending on the wind. Take the self-guided nature trails through the dunes, and you can make it all the way to the Roanoke Sound side of the Outer Banks, where you'll find a swimming beach. The park is known for its strong winds, so kite flying and hang gliding are two popular activities here.

It's all about the view at San Francisco's Baker Beach. The mile-long stretch of sand has direct sight lines of the nearby Golden Gate Bridge, not to mention views of the Marin Headlands beyond. The dog-friendly and family-friendly beach is often filled with sunbathers, picnickers, and grillers taking full advantage of the park's facilities. Just be aware that this isn't a great swimming beach, as the waters are rough here. There are hikes all around the beach, including the California Coastal Trail and the Batteries to Bluffs Trail, which are connected by a challenging climb called the Sand Ladder.

BAKER BEACH	San Francisco, California	UNITED STATES OF AMERICA

Some two-thirds of the island of Saint John is protected by Virgin Islands National Park, and that includes gorgeous Trunk Bay, one of the most beautiful beaches in the Caribbean. There's about a quarter mile of white sand on this beach that's perfect for sunbathing, but the real gem is actually in the water. Grab your snorkel mask and fins and make for the Underwater Snorkel Trail, a 400-foot trail with signage interpreting sea life around you, from coral formations to endemic fish species.

	**TRUNK BAY**	Saint John, U.S. Virgin Islands	UNITED STATES OF AMERICA

If you've ever wanted to go swimming in Utah's Great Salt Lake, you can go for it with gusto at Bridger Bay Beach in Antelope Island State Park. The water off the white-sand beach is quite shallow, but if you wade out far enough, you'll see just how buoyant you are in this high-salinity water—it's far saltier than the ocean. The park is also a great place to take in the desert landscape and all its inhabitants, from the namesake antelope of the island to bison to waterfowl.

BRIDGER BAY BEACH	Antelope Island State Park, Utah	UNITED STATES OF AMERICA

HONOKALANI BEACH

Wai‘ānapanapa State Park, Maui, Hawaii

UNITED STATES OF AMERICA

While the Big Island of Hawaii is renowned for its black-sand beaches, Maui has a small one, too. Honokalani Beach in Waiʻānapanapa State Park is a black-sand beach along the island's famous Road to Hana. Swimming is advisable only if the sea is especially calm, which doesn't happen too often here. Instead, spend your time sunning yourself on the sand, watching the glistening water, and listening to the sounds of nature. Or put some hiking shoes on and explore the rugged coastline's rock formations and lava tubes, looking for seabird colonies along the way. Keep in mind that visitors to the state park will need an advance reservation to enter.

	SHARM EL LULI	Wadi El Gemal National Park	EGYPT

About a 45-minute drive south of the resort town of Marsa Alam on Egypt's Red Sea coast is Sharm El Luli, a secluded beach famous for its soft sands, rocky outcrops, and turquoise waters. Because it's located within Wadi El Gemal National Park, there's no development here—it's just pristine nature. As such, this is a prime snorkeling spot, with reefs just off the beach filled with colorful fish and sea turtles. Just be sure to pack everything you need for a beach day, since there are no beach clubs, gear rental facilities, or, well, any sort of infrastructure here. And that's precisely what makes it a great beach!

Kenya certainly has a reputation as a safari hotspot, but for those craving some downtime at the beach, the country also has a stunning coastline along the Indian Ocean. Diani Beach is a popular beach destination about an hour south of Mombasa, and it's not hard to see why—with miles of white sand fringed by lush forests, this beach looks like a postcard. Book a stay at a local resort at the end of a safari, then try your hand at kitesurfing or don a snorkel and extend your wildlife vacation underwater. Or simply relax at a beach restaurant with a cocktail in hand.

	DIANI BEACH	Kwale County	KENYA

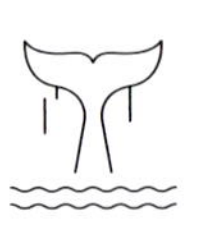

ANDILANA	Nosy Be	MADAGASCAR

Just off the northern tip of Madagascar is the resort island of Nosy Be, a tropical paradise for beach lovers—and fragrance lovers, too, as the island is known for its ylang-ylang plantations. The white-sand Andilana beach has both public and private sections, the latter reserved for the destination's beach resorts. While the beach itself is best for sunbathing, land sports, and swimming, the waters here are not necessarily the best snorkeling on the island. But Nosy Be as a whole is a prime spot to snorkel with whale sharks, so be sure to book an excursion during your vacation here.

Nosy Komba is a small volcanic island between mainland Madagascar and Nosy Be, and it has one iconic claim to fame: lemurs. In fact, "Nosy Komba" means "island of lemurs" in Malagasy, the local language. The island's forested interior is full of them, so you'll likely see at least a few on a trip here. But you're here for the beaches, and there are plenty of those surrounding the island, off which you'll find thriving coral reefs for snorkeling. The island's lodges and resorts make for the perfect home base to explore the adjacent Nosy Tanikely Marine National Park, including the tiny Nosy Tanikely, which has its own beautiful beach.

	**NOSY KOMBA**	Nosy Be	MADAGASCAR

NOSY TSARABANJINA

Mitsio Archipelago

MADAGASCAR

Madagascar's Nosy Tsarabanjina is a private island in the Mitsio Archipelago, home to the luxury eco-resort Constance Tsarabanjina. There are 25 thatched-roof bungalows with direct beach access, the Indian Ocean's azure waters just steps from your bed. The resort provides guests with snorkel gear, kayaks, and stand-up paddleboards so you can explore the island's various beaches at your leisure. There's also a dive center for those who want to spend even more time underwater; one of the most popular dive sites here is Les Quatre Frères, or the four brothers, which are rocky islets filled with seabirds just offshore.

POSTE LAFAYETTE BEACH

Rivière du Rempart

MAURITIUS

Unlike the bustling tourist beaches of northwest Mauritius, Poste Lafayette Beach on the island's east coast is a spot for nature lovers. Here, waves crash against black lava rocks, between which are sandy stretches dotted with mangrove trees. The windy conditions make this a popular kitesurfing and windsurfing spot, though the rough seas aren't exactly ideal for swimming or snorkeling. If adventure watersports aren't your jam, pack a picnic lunch, sit in the shade of a mangrove, and simply watch the show! If you'd like to base your vacation here, there are a number of resorts and villa rentals along the coast.

The small town of Trou-aux-Biches in Mauritius might've started as a humble fishing village, but today it's a laid-back resort destination celebrated for its long, white-sand beach with calm, shallow waters. Several luxury hotels, such as Trou aux Biches Beachcomber, line the shore, providing excellent amenities for a relaxing beach holiday. As Trou-aux-Biches beach faces west, it's a popular spot for sunset strolls—or you can book dinner at a beachfront restaurant to take in nature's evening show. During the day, however, it's worth booking a snorkeling excursion or even a submarine ride to see sea turtles.

	**TROU-AUX-BICHES**	Pamplemousses	MAURITIUS

	**GRAND BAIE**	Rivière du Rempart	MAURITIUS

If it's amenities you seek at your Mauritius beach, the public beach Grand Baie is the perfect option for you. This is a bustling beach rather than a quiet sanctuary, as it's located right next to a tourist hub of the same name—but that means there are plenty of activities here, from watersports rentals to catamaran cruises to deep-sea fishing tours. Plus, there's easy access to restaurants and bars for entertainment. Beyond the main beach, there are also smaller public beaches in town, including La Cuvette and Pereybere, which might offer a little more peace and quiet than the main beach.

Between Madagascar and Mozambique, just east of the Comoros, you'll find the French overseas territory of Mayotte. The baobab-lined N'Gouja Beach, located on the southern coast of the island, is a marine life hotspot—the beach is known for its resident sea turtles, which can often be seen grazing on seagrass in the calm, shallow waters. If you swim out past the seagrass, you'll reach the coral reef, where more underwater fauna awaits. For the most convenient access to this beach, stay at the boutique eco-lodge Le Jardin Maore, located right on the lagoon. The hotel also has a dive center that can organize excursions across the island.

	**N'GOUJA BEACH**	Kani-Kéli	MAYOTTE

Sometimes it's not the sand that's the most interesting thing about the beach. Sometimes it's the sand*stone*. Legzira Beach, located near the town of Sidi Ifni on Morocco's Atlantic coast, is famous for its dramatic red sandstone cliffs, including a giant stone arch eroded by the wind and waves over centuries. (There used to be a second arch here, but it collapsed in 2016, demonstrating the ephemerality of the fragile stone.) While the beach is relatively remote and quiet, it's a favorite among adventure enthusiasts, namely surfers, windsurfers, and kitesurfers, who take advantage of the sea conditions here.

	LEGZIRA BEACH	Sidi Ifni	MOROCCO

INHACA ISLAND	Maputo	MOZAMBIQUE

For travelers spending time in Maputo, Mozambique, the nearby Inhaca Island is a must-visit, whether on a day trip or for an extended stay at one of its lodges or resorts. The beach-lined island is a hub for biodiversity both above and below the water; it's a popular destination for birdwatching, with many species native to the island, but Inhaca is also known for its coral reefs filled with such sea life as potato groupers and barracudas. Whale sharks and manta rays are another draw to Inhaca's waters. Whether you choose to bird-watch on the beach with binoculars or snorkel with finned friends, you're sure to have a wildlife-filled adventure here.

Bazaruto Island, the largest island in Mozambique's Bazaruto Archipelago, is renowned for its stunning white-sand beaches, towering dunes, and crystal-clear waters. As one of five islands in the Bazaruto Archipelago National Park, this ecosystem is highly protected, and that means it's an ideal spot for wildlife. The island's most famous residents are dugongs—here you'll find the last-known viable dugong population in East Africa. But they're not the only animals benefiting from the protective measures in the national park. The waters here are also home to dolphins, whales, sharks, marlins, and sea turtles.

	BAZARUTO ISLAND	Bazaruto Archipelago	MOZAMBIQUE

SANDWICH HARBOUR

Namib-Naukluft National Park

NAMIBIA

Namibia might be known for its deserts, but in Sandwich Harbour, wildlife thrives. Here, monumental sand dunes tumble down into the sea, where wetlands support quite active birdlife. Sandwich Harbour is located within Namib-Naukluft National Park in Namibia, some 30 miles south of Walvis Bay, and although it's difficult to access by car, guided 4×4 tours can take visitors across the dunes to witness the spectacular meeting of sand and sea. At low tide, 4×4s can even drive right along the surf—keep an eye out for dolphins as you're zipping along.

SKELETON COAST NATIONAL PARK

—

NAMIBIA

The Skeleton Coast is one of the most remote and rugged beach destinations in the world, running for hundreds of miles in northwest Namibia. The foreboding name is derived from the more than 1,000 shipwrecks along the shore—conditions here are unforgivable, particularly when blinding fog blurs the line between sea and desert dunes. While sailors might have dubbed the Skeleton Coast "the Gates of Hell," it's a pretty spectacular place to visit, especially for photographers looking to capture the stark landscape and the old metal bones of long-dead ships.

ANSE SOURCE D'ARGENT	La Digue	SEYCHELLES

The island of La Digue is one of the Seychelles' inner granitic islands, and when you visit its most popular beach, Anse Source d'Argent, you'll really come to understand the term "granitic." The pink-sand beach is lined with giant granite boulders, well worn by the ocean over many years. While the beach is open to the public, you'll enter it through L'Union Estate, a former coconut and vanilla plantation, which has an entry fee that goes toward protecting the area. While facilities are limited on the beach itself, there are often fruit vendors peddling rejuvenating treats to beachgoers.

ANSE LAZIO	Praslin	SEYCHELLES

Praslin's Anse Lazio might draw comparisons to La Digue's Anse Source d'Argent, thanks to the proliferation of giant granite boulders along the shore, but it's worthy of a visit in its own right. Because it's much larger than Anse Source d'Argent, there's much more space to spread out. Bring a big beach blanket for lounging on the powdery white sand and a snorkel mask to see what fish you might spot in the calm cerulean waters. And when you're in need of some refreshments, you can visit one of the beach bars or restaurants for an ice-cold drink.

	**ANSE GEORGETTE**	Praslin	SEYCHELLES

Anse Georgette, another gem on Praslin, offers a more secluded and intimate experience compared with the busier beaches in Seychelles. The fairly petite beach in a crescent-shaped cove is surrounded by verdant hills and—you guessed it—granite boulders. It's accessed via the Constance Lemuria resort, most commonly by guests, but also by members of the general public (inform the resort of your wish to visit the beach in advance, as admission is limited). Be prepared for a bit of a trek to the beach, as the path from the main resort winds through the golf course before making it down to the sand.

	BEAU VALLON BEACH	Mahé	SEYCHELLES

Not all of the Seychelles' beaches are remote stretches of sand. Beau Vallon Beach, for instance, is one of the busiest beaches in the archipelago, but still one of the most beautiful. Located near the capital city Victoria on the island of Mahé, this long, wide beach has a number of hotels along it, with restaurants, bars, and beach clubs. And while there's plenty to do on shore, there's plenty to do in the water, too. Look for watersports rentals and dive centers, or simply go for a swim in the warm, turquoise sea.

	COFFEE BAY	Wild Coast	SOUTH AFRICA

When you think of a "hole in the wall," you might picture a dive bar or a greasy spoon. But in Coffee Bay, the hole in the wall is literal—there's a sea cliff here with a famous hole right in the middle of it, carved out by the waves. The beach here is one of many on South Africa's Wild Coast of the Eastern Cape, some of which have golden sands, others of which are pebbly. While you can relax on the beach, you'll find most visitors pursuing more vigorous activities, such as hiking along the coastline or surfing when there's a good swell.

	CAMPS BAY BEACH	Camps Bay	SOUTH AFRICA

With a backdrop of the Twelve Apostles mountain range, Camps Bay is a pretty beautiful beach from a purely visual point of view. But it's also Cape Town's party beach. The white sands are bordered by a bustling promenade with beach bars, restaurants, clubs, and hotels—it's quite the scene during the summer. As the Atlantic waters can be chilly, most beachgoers remain on the sand, though brave individuals might take a quick dip to cool down. For calmer and potentially warmer waters, venture down to the Camps Bay Tidal Pool, a human-made swimming spot built into the rocks of the beach.

GONUBIE BEACH	East London	SOUTH AFRICA

Just outside of the South African city of East London, Gonubie Beach is a quiet and family-friendly beach where the Gonubie River meets the sea, and it's known for its wide sandy shores. The beach has Blue Flag status, which ensures high quality and safety standards, and that means Gonubie is ideal for swimming in both the sea and the human-made tidal pool. There's also a boardwalk that traverses the beach along the base of the sand dunes. Grab a seat on one of the boardwalk's benches and gaze out at the water—you never know if you might see a whale or a dolphin.

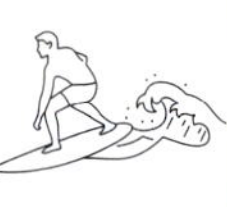	LONG BEACH	Kommetjie	SOUTH AFRICA

If you like long walks on the beach, you might just like Long Beach in the Cape Town suburb of Kommetjie. The beach is indeed long, and it's a favorite for hikers thanks to its scenic trails: popular sites include the *SS Kakapo* shipwreck from 1900 and the Slangkop Lighthouse, from which you can enjoy panoramic views of the mountainous coastline. Because this beach faces west, it's rather exposed to the Atlantic—and that makes for excellent surfing. Or for the more leisurely inclined, this is also a birding hotspot, so bring your binoculars.

All the way at the northern tip of Zanzibar is Nungwi, a vibrant beach destination offering a blend of natural beauty, cultural experiences, and lively nightlife. Sure, Nungwi Beach is known for its white sand and brilliant blue water, not to mention the traditional dhow boats along the shore—the combination leads to some pretty photographable moments. But the beach is also known for watersports from surfing to diving. And once the sun goes down, you'll find the beachgoers leaving the sand for the beach bars, restaurants, and clubs, where the party will last all night long.

NUNGWI BEACH	Zanzibar	TANZANIA

	KENDWA BEACH	Zanzibar	TANZANIA

The (slightly) more laid-back sister to Nungwi Beach, the resort-laden Kendwa Beach in Zanzibar is a top spot for swimming. Why? Because the white-sand beach is not very affected by tides, the water level remains fairly consistent. Plus, the beach is also protected from winds, meaning the waters are often quite calm. As it's located on the west side of the island, Kendwa Beach has incredible sunset views, making for a romantic evening stroll or dinner at one of the beach restaurants. And every month, the beach comes to life with a Full Moon Party.

Mnemba Island, a private island off the northeast coast of Zanzibar that is home to andBeyond Mnemba Island Lodge, is a dreamy beach getaway. The island, which has a circumference of less than a mile, is completely ringed by a white-sand beach, while nearby sandbanks provide more room for exploration. The island is actually a coral atoll, which means it's surrounded by a very active reef—and it's also an important nesting site for green turtles. While snorkeling is always an option, there's a dive center here that caters to all, from novices to experts.

	MNEMBA BEACH	Zanzibar	TANZANIA

	**DECEPTION ISLAND**	—	SOUTH SHETLAND ISLANDS

Beaches aren't found only in tropical destinations. Even icy Antarctica is home to beaches! Take, for instance, Deception Island in the South Shetland Islands, just off the coast of the Antarctic Peninsula. This horseshoe-shaped volcanic island has black-sand beaches, with steam often rising from the shallow waters of its caldera to remind you of the geothermal activities happening below ground. (The last major eruption was in 1970.) Visitors to Deception Island can explore an abandoned whaling station, hike to scenic overlooks for breathtaking views across the natural harbor, and wander among penguins and seals.

	**ST. ANDREWS BAY**	—	SOUTH GEORGIA

South Georgia, a mountainous Atlantic island with ties to Antarctica, has numerous beaches along its craggy shores. One of its most famous is St. Andrews Bay, where a wide plain along the sea is home to 150,000 mating pairs of king penguins—this is certainly the largest king penguin colony in South Georgia. Beyond the kings, there are also elephant seals and fur seals here, making for a true wildlife spectacle. Of course, because most of the real estate is taken up by animals, this isn't much of a beach for sunbathing or swimming. Plus, it's fairly cold here in the summer, anyway.

Credits
All images © iStock

p. 10 Lovleah
p. 12 tomograf
p. 14 SRFlorisson
p. 16 Hideaki Edo
p. 18 Allen Dartnell
p. 20 Andrew Peacock
p. 22 autau
p. 24 byrneck
p. 26 AshR
p. 28 Photon-Photos
p. 30 DarrenTierney
p. 32 DarrenTierney
p. 34 Mlenny
p. 36 mvaligursky
p. 38 SteveAllenPhoto
p. 40 AsianDream
p. 42 Ed-Ni-Photo
p. 44 Martin Vlnas
p. 46 Dirschl
p. 48 Michael Schollum
p. 50 natmint
p. 52 Kerry Hargrove
p. 53 Wirestock
p. 54 Stewart Watson
p. 56 jlazouphoto
p. 58 corners74
p. 60 Dmitry Malov
p. 62 bjeayes
p. 63 cyoshi
p. 64 mvaligursky
p. 66 rweisswald
p. 67 livcool
p. 68 Wirestock
p. 70 Diy13
p. 72 laytonjeff
p. 73 Wirestock
p. 74 cinoby
p. 76 wallix
p. 78 Skazzjy
p. 79 Mlenny
p. 80 Mlenny
p. 82 bymuratdeniz
p. 84 fbxx
p. 86 Eduardo Cabanas
p. 88 leolintang
p. 90 gyro
p. 92 7maru
p. 94 DoctorEgg
p. 96 AsianDream
p. 98 Ts Yew
p. 100 xtremesailing
p. 102 photoaliona
p. 104 Mary Grace Varela
p. 106 Mary Grace Varela
p. 108 Andrey Danilovich
p. 109 danilovi
p. 110 Evgenyi_Eg
p. 112 Besides the Obvious
p. 114 Besides the Obvious
p. 116 Dmitrii Anikin
p. 118 Aurore Kervoern
p. 119 Aurore Kervoern
p. 120 Rabyesang
p. 122 Preto_perola
p. 124 Preto_perola
p. 126 Pierrick Lemaret
p. 128 Pierrick Lemaret
p. 130 Drablenkov
p. 132 Drablenkov
p. 134 frantic00
p. 136 ardasavasciogullari
p. 138 HuyThoai
p. 140 FG Trade
p. 142 Balate Dorin
p. 144 Janoka82
p. 146 encrier
p. 148 dmbaker
p. 149 CaptureLight
p. 150 CaptureLight
p. 152 olrat
p. 154 Kerrick
p. 156 PK-Photos
p. 157 PK-Photos
p. 158 Mariusz Pietranek
p. 160 borchee
p. 162 pidjoe
p. 164 janiecbros
p. 166 Pilat666
p. 168 Ana del Castillo
p. 170 Nisangha
p. 172 Martin Diebel
p. 174 Mlenny
p. 176 ezypix
p. 178 Agnieszka Glowala
p. 179 KucherAV
p. 180 marako85
p. 182 Michael Gill
p. 184 Nadtochiy
p. 186 CreativeNature_nl
p. 188 tunart
p. 190 katerinasergeevna
p. 190 ruivalesousa
p. 194 katatonia82
p. 195 katatonia82
p. 196 Artur Bogacki
p. 198 Wirestock
p. 200 Julen Arabaolaza
p. 202 DieterMeyrl
p. 204 Manel Vinuesa
p. 206 daboost
p. 207 samuel howell
p. 208 Inigo Arza Azcorra
p. 210 Worledit
p. 212 Jessica Belliere
p. 213 YassminKa
p. 214 KavalenkavaVolha

p. 216 Photosbypatrik
p. 217 Martin Wahlborg
p. 218 Jimi Zen
p. 220 acceleratorhams
p. 222 Roddy Mc Dowall
p. 224 AlasdairJames
p. 226 colbourne49
p. 228 Jitchanamont
p. 230 Richard Heath
p. 232 AlexPhotoStock
p. 234 marchello74
p. 236 marchello74
p. 238 microgen
p. 240 Thomas De Wever
p. 242 Phaelnogueira
p. 244 Anderson Spinelli
p. 246 MesquitaFMS
p. 248 MaFelipe
p. 250 JP Carnevalli
p. 252 JeremyRichards
p. 254 abriendomundo
p. 256 Judith Engbers
p. 258 Boarding1Now
p. 260 tifonimages
p. 262 CStorz
p. 264 RPBMedia
p. 266 guenterguni
p. 268 holgs
p. 270 Jennifer Bachman
p. 272 fotoquique
p. 274 Solange_Z
p. 276 Wirestock
p. 278 Cristian Lourenço
p. 280 sHansche
p. 282 BriBar
p. 284 ChiragYadav
p. 286 Panya_
p. 288 vale_t
p. 290 sbonk
p. 292 Sven Thilo
p. 294 Alexis Gonzalez
p. 296 Mary Baratto
p. 298 gqxue
p. 300 Cheng Feng Chiang
p. 302 mikolajn
p. 304 holgs
p. 306 AutumnSkyPhotography
p. 308 Caroline Brundle Bugge
p. 310 Fertnig
p. 312 czekma13
p. 314 valio84sl
p. 316 Nandani Bridglal
p. 318 wwing
p. 320 Simon Dannhauer
p. 322 Elijah-Lovkoff
p. 324 eddygaleotti
p. 326 shalamov
p. 328 Mary Baratto
p. 330 fokkebok
p. 332 Valerie Loiseleux
p. 334 Noah Zastrow
p. 336 vale_t
p. 338 shalamov
p. 340 raksyBH
p. 342 Pgiam
p. 344 Art Wager
p. 346 Ed Williams
p. 348 Wirestock
p. 350 AndrewSoundarajan
p. 352 pchoui
p. 354 jimkruger
p. 356 campeong
p. 358 Chris Domingo
p. 359 fusaromike
p. 360 Luckohnen
p. 362 Tomas Kozak
p. 364 Haizhan Zheng
p. 366 DenisTangneyJr
p. 368 AppalachianViews
p. 370 pawel.gaul
p. 372 felixmizioznikov
p. 374 cipella
p. 375 vanillastring
p. 376 Philippe Fleury
p. 378 Kyle Little
p. 380 lucky-photographer
p. 382 cdwheatley
p. 384 Aubrey Banning
p. 386 Mlenny
p. 388 Ibrahim Hamroush
p. 390 solidcolours
p. 392 Eduardo Cabanas
p. 394 Ava-Leigh
p. 396 pierivb
p. 398 steve-goacher
p. 400 Tomasz Banaczek
p. 402 Balate Dorin
p. 403 Africanway
p. 404 Insularis
p. 406 mmeee
p. 408 wildacad
p. 410 demerzel21
p. 412 demerzel21
p. 414 Pascale Gueret
p. 416 Pavel Mora
p. 418 Diamond Dogs
p. 420 Aleh Varanishcha
p. 421 Delpixart
p. 422 ChristianB
p. 424 PJPhoto69
p. 426 ~UserGI15667539
p. 428 Ameen Ryland
p. 431 ToscaWhi
p. 432 ZambeziShark
p. 433 David Robinson
p. 434 Robertobinetti70
p. 436 laranik
p. 438 den-belitsky
p. 439 den-belitsky
p. 440 den-belitsky
p. 442 kitz-travellers
p. 444 elmvilla
backcover valio84sl

TEXT
Stefanie Waldek

BOOK DESIGN / COVER ILLUSTRATION
Han van de Ven

EDITING
Léa Teuscher

Sign up for our newsletter with news about new and forthcoming publications on art, interior design, food and travel, photography and fashion as well as exclusive offers and events. If you have any questions or comments about the material in this book, please do not hesitate to contact our editorial team: art@lannoo.com.

D/2024/45/189 - NUR 450/500
ISBN: 978 94 014 9895 1

www.lannoo.com